A BARTHOLOMEW MAP & GUIDE

WALK THE COTSWOLDS

BY JILL BROWN & DAVID SKELHON

JOHN BARTHOLOMEW & SON LTD
EDINBURGH

British Library Cataloguing in Publication Data
Brown, Jill
Walk the Cotswolds
1. England. Cotswolds — Visitors' guides
I. Title II. Skelhon, David
914.24'1704858
ISBN 0–7028–0908–x

Published and Printed in Scotland
by John Bartholomew & Son Ltd.,
Duncan Street, Edinburgh EH9 1TA

First edition 1989

Produced for John Bartholomew & Son Ltd
by Curtis Garratt Limited, The Old Vicarage,
Horton cum Studley, Oxford OX9 1BT

Typesetting and maps by Taurus Graphics

Layouts by Taurus Graphics

ISBN 0 7028 0908 x

CONTENTS

KEY MAP FOR THE WALKS

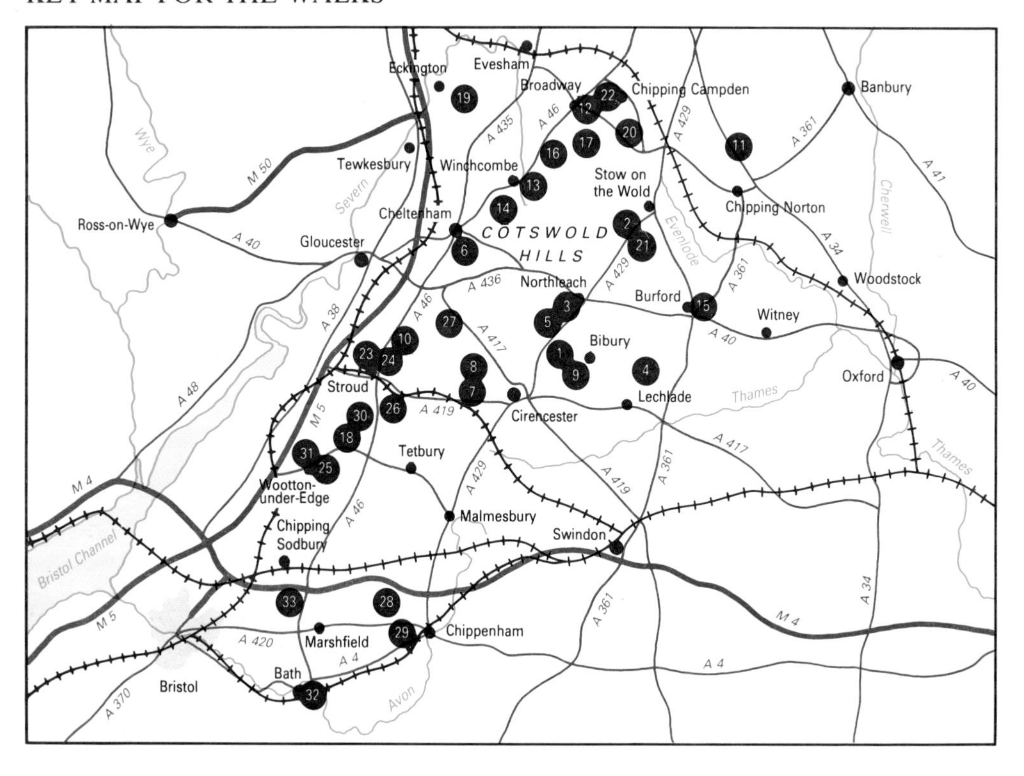

KEY TO SCALE AND MAP SYMBOLS

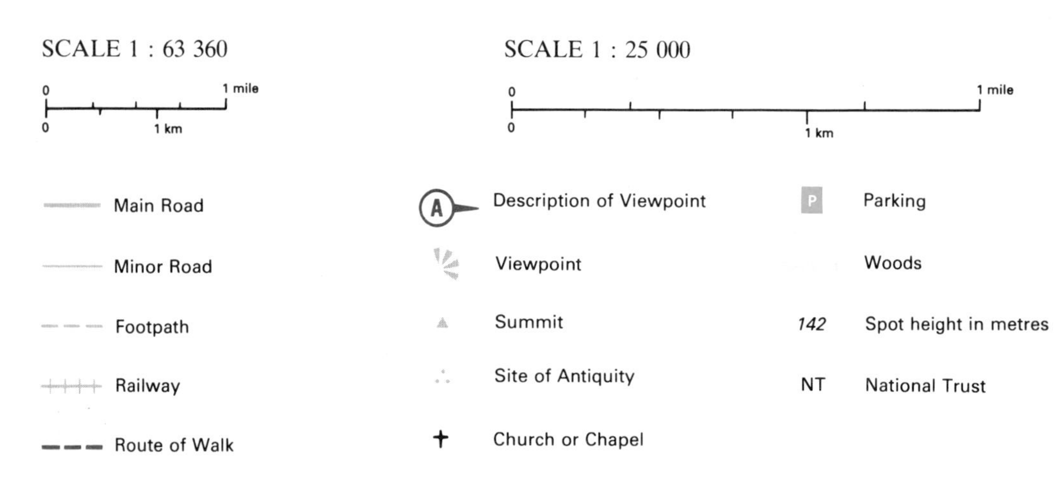

1 WHY WALK THE COTSWOLDS?

There are many areas of Britain with individual character but the Cotswolds must stand as one of the most distinctive, with an unmistakable charm and atmosphere all its own.

A unique set of natural and historical events has shaped the scenery we see today, and has bestowed a rich visual heritage upon the landscape. The Cotswolds have much to offer the visitor prepared to don a pair of boots for they are best savoured slowly, and those wandering through them at walking pace stand to gain the most from their experience.

This is not remote or wild upland country and those familiar with such places would probably class this more as lowland walking. Indeed, unlike the high moors, people are not intruders here but rather have enhanced the landscape by skilful use of the resource at their feet.

For many visitors, the most memorable impression of the Cotswolds is the mellow stone which seems visually to bind the countryside together. Stone is the very fabric of the place, and so suitable a material that the houses seem to grow out of the ground. Its varying hues of yellow, cream, gold, and brown are often covered with a frosting of lichen, and inspired J B Priestley to say that the walls know 'the trick of keeping the lost sunlight of centuries glimmering upon them'.

The stone was used as long ago as Neolithic folk to bury their dead, but by far the most prodigious building period began during the Middle Ages, funded by the growth of the wool trade. The wool merchants made their fortunes and lavished some of their immense wealth on the construction of homes and churches. The result is an outstanding legacy of domestic and religious architecture in a region where even the humblest barn or outbuilding seems to have been constructed originally with a degree of masonic pride.

Had the prosperity continued, we would doubtless have come into a different inheritance. Ironically, it was the decline of the cloth trade, beginning in the eighteenth century, and an agricultural depression in the nineteenth that discouraged further development, enabling whole towns and villages to survive largely unspoilt into the twentieth century.

Lovely as they are, the villages are but one element in the Cotswold scene, and the landscape itself varies between the gentler eastern wolds and the dramatic western Edge. From the escarpment, there are wonderful unobstructed views to the west and north affording sweeping panoramas over the Severn Vale and the Vale of Evesham.

It can seem that the hordes of summer visitors spoil the scenery but, as elsewhere, they tend to concentrate in the well-known 'honey pots', leaving the surrounding countryside to the locals or the cognoscenti. Those out for a quiet stroll need not despair for there are still many quiet corners, and the walker has a choice of itinerary to suit his or her mood.

Both the famous and the not-so-well-known aspects of the Cotswolds are included in this book but, in the space available, it can only be a selective guide to some of the finest and the best that the area offers. The hope is that it will encourage further personal exploration and lead to a greater appreciation of this unique environmental heritage.

2 CLOTHING AND EQUIPMENT

Comfortable footwear is vital and, for the Cotswolds, lightweight leather boots with good tread for slippery slopes are ideal. For short walks on wet or muddy ground the underrated wellington can be particularly useful.

Waterproof jackets and trousers are important, not only for protection from showers but also for warmth on windswept ridges and heights. Overtrousers are also useful when walking through wet vegetation. In the colder months a hat will conserve a lot of warmth because up to a third of body heat is lost through an uncovered head.

It is important to carry a compass, preferably one of the 'Silva' type and, of course, the relevant map. Binoculars are not essential but are very useful for spotting distant stiles and give added interest to viewpoints and wildlife. A pair of 8 x 30s are powerful enough but still light enough to be carried comfortably.

Finally, these items can best be carried in a lightweight daysack.

3 PUBLIC RIGHTS OF WAY

In England and Wales rights of way fall into three main categories:

(a) Public Footpaths – for walkers only
(b) Bridleways – for passage on foot, horseback, or bicycle
(c) Byways – for all the above and for motorized vehicles

The Highway Authorities are usually responsible for the maintenance of rights of way in their area and are able to take action against offending landowners.

They are also responsible for the upkeep of definitive maps which show public rights of way. A right of way exists as long as it is on the definitive map. The maps are usually kept at county or district council offices.

A walker may linger to admire the view or eat lunch but must not obstruct a right of way. It is up to walkers to ensure that they keep to the designated path for, if they wander away from it – either deliberately or unintentionally – they may be trespassing and the landowner is entitled to sue. The trespassing walker must leave the land immediately if asked to do so by the landowner.

Sooner or later a walker is likely to come across a path blocked by an obstruction. You have the right to remove it just enough to pass by but you cannot go on to a right of way with prior knowledge of an obstruction and the intention to remove it.

Growing crops are the most common obstruction, and you are entitled to walk through them even if this means that some damage is unavoidable. This is often unpleasant and with mature crops virtually impossible. You may, in these circumstances, go around the crop but it is advisable to stay within the field boundary to avoid trespass on someone else's land.

A farmer can plough up a public footpath but must usually reinstate it within two weeks. The farmer is not normally permitted to plough up a footpath which runs along the edge of the field.

The presence of a bull alongside a path can be unnerving but not necessarily illegal, for a farmer may turn out a mature beef bull as long as there are cows present. Dairy bulls, the most common being the Friesian, are illegal, and the walker must be extremely wary of them. In practice, though, it may be difficult for the untrained eye to distinguish between beef and dairy breeds.

Dogs are allowed on public rights of way if they are under close control. You are liable to prosecution and the dog may be shot if it is found worrying farm animals.

4 THE COUNTRY CODE

The country code can be summed up with the well-known adage 'leave only footprints, take only photographs'. It only takes a little care and thought. Don't, for instance, drop litter – fluorescent orange peel, crushed drink cans, and brightly coloured chocolate wrappers do not blend well with the environment.

Shut all gates and use the proper stiles to cross walls and hedges. On narrow paths walk in single file to avoid unnecessary erosion.

Do not disturb the wildlife, and remember that the Wildlife and Countryside Act of 1981 gives strong protection to many wild creatures. Many plants have special protection and must not be picked intentionally. In any case, flowers are there for all to enjoy.

The country code is based on common sense and you will offend no one if you leave the countryside as you found it.

5 MAP READING

Maps convey a considerable amount of information to the experienced eye, and navigational skills should be acquired by all who wander through the countryside.

The most useful scale of map for the walker is the 1:25 000 or 2½ inches to the mile. Features are shown in greater detail than on the 1:50 000 maps, and all public rights of way are easily identifiable in green ink. Most of all, they show field boundaries, which are very useful for determining the route of a path.

Failure to identify your current position correctly is often the first step in becoming lost. To confirm your position, simply orientate the map with the compass so that the grid of the map lies in line with the needle, which should point to the top of the map. Recognizable landmarks should then relate to those on the map, as will other minor features.

Remember that it is easy to make mistakes and maps do become quickly out of date – hedges are grubbed up, footpaths are diverted. Do not become too carried away with the scenery or overestimate your navigational ability, and make frequent checks on your position.

6 THE PHYSICAL STRUCTURE

The Cotswolds are part of a great belt of limestone that stretches from Lincoln to Dorset. They are often referred to as hills, a misleading and inaccurate term because there is no range of hills as such but rather a plateau of generally medium altitude, most of which lies between 400 and 800 feet (120–240 metres). This has been tilted gently to the south-east with the higher, north-western edge forming a distinct and sometimes dramatic boundary.

Elsewhere, the limits of the Cotswolds are more difficult to define. The stone belt continues south into Somerset and Dorset and, to the east, merges gradually into the meadowlands of the Thames. The northern boundary is even harder to determine, and Cotswold country could be said to extend as far as Edgehill.

The western scarp is highest and steepest in its northern and middle sections, reaching over 1000 feet (300 m) between Cheltenham and Broadway. It may rise 600 feet (180 m) in less than a mile (1.6 km) while the gentle dip slope continues east for up to 20 miles (32 km).

At times, the Edge is fairly straight, but elsewhere it has been convoluted by dissecting river valleys, such as around Bath and Stroud.

These west-flowing streams have steep gradients, up to 1 in 10, and nearly all flow to the Severn. The southern end of the Cotswolds lies in the Avon catchment, but by far the largest area is drained by the Thames in the north-east. Here it collects the waters of the longer, more spacious rivers that flow over the dip slope in more or less parallel valleys running north-west to south-east.

It is evident from detached outliers, such as Bredon Hill, that the limestone once covered a larger area than at present. The scarp slope has receded south-eastwards under the onslaught of erosion that has caused portions of limestone to fall down as the softer rocks underneath have been eaten away.

The distinct, isolated hills now standing in the Severn Vale are mainly the work of streams that have cut back their headwaters into the limestone. Where the stream has been powerful enough, it has isolated the hill from the main plateau. This has already happened to Cam Long Down, Robins Wood Hill, and Churchdown, and will soon occur at Stinchcombe Hill, where the tongue of land is connected to the main mass by a ridge only a few hundred yards wide.

Another feature of the Cotswolds are the curiously dry valleys. These may have been cut when the water table was much higher or by powerful streams of meltwater at the end of the Ice Age when the ground was still frozen.

The rocks

The foundations of the Cotswolds were laid down during the Jurassic era some 170 to 100 million years ago when the area lay under the sea and enjoyed a subtropical climate. There was also abundant plant and animal life, and many of the rocks contain fossils.

Although the limestone is the best known of the rocks, it occurs in a series with sands and muds. Very broadly, the clays underlie the plains, the sands form the foothills, and the limestone forms the highest ground.

The limestone is not a uniform rock, varying in colour and composition throughout the area. Geologists have identified two main types, with the older Inferior Oolite underlying the younger Great Oolite.

The Great Oolite once probably overlaid the whole of the Cotswolds, but much of it was eroded away after the area was raised and tilted to the south-east. Consequently, today it is found on the dip slope between about 600 and 800 feet and (180–240 m) while the Inferior Oolite covers the highest land above 800 feet (240 m).

The Inferior Oolite is composed mainly of rounded spheres of calcium carbonate. These so resemble the roe of a fish that the rock has been named from the Greek *oios lithos* meaning 'egg stone'. It has provided some fine building stone, such as that from the quarry at Leckhampton, but it varies in quality. In places, it consists largely of shell fragments, in which cases it has proved very suitable for dry stone walling.

The Great Oolite is a hard white rock that is classed among the finest of building materials. The famous Bath Stone, for example, was used at Blenheim, Eton, and Windsor Castle. It was mined from inclined shafts, a convenient method because the stone had to be protected from frost when freshly dug during winter. A maze of storage tunnels surrounded the quarries, and between Box and Corsham, for instance, it is estimated that there are about 60 miles (97 km) of underground galleries.

Between the two limestones are layers of fuller's earth and Stonesfield Slate – two more rocks that have played an important part in the history and appearance of the Cotswolds.

Fuller's earth was used for cleansing wool and felting cloth. Stonesfield Slate is a fissile, sandy limestone found in the north and mid-Cotswolds. It is the traditional tiling material used throughout history since Neolithic times, and forms the characteristic lichen-covered roofs that are features of Cotswold architecture in themselves.

At one time, almost every village had its own quarry. The industry has greatly declined with competition from cheaper materials, however, and very few quarries are now in operation.

7 HUMAN HISTORY

Mesolithic man probably hunted along the scarp after the end of the last Ice Age, preferring the higher, drier ground to the marshy vale below.

These people left few relics but the next wave of settlers gave us lasting memorials. Neolithic farmers crossed the Channel from the Mediterranean around 3500 BC, bringing with them their animals and building techniques. These are the people who constructed the long barrows, with a design that was distinctive enough to have been named 'the Severn-Cotswold type'. They were burial places for important individuals and their families, and must have involved considerable organization and effort. At an average of 100 to 200 feet (30–60 m) long and up to 18 feet (5.5 m) high, they would have taken thousands of man hours to construct as well as thousands of tons of stone – all quarried with antler picks.

The earlier barrows have a true entrance, and the later ones a false portal flanked by curving horns of dry stone walling. There is hardly any difference between this ancient stonework and modern walling, representing an amazing historical continuity of 4000 years.

Later Beaker immigrants cremated their dead and interred them in round barrows, relatively insignificant structures in comparison. They were followed by the Celtic Iron Age people, who constructed the hillforts along the escarpment. At first, they were built with single ramparts, but later they developed multiple defences, possibly a reaction to the increasing use of the sling. They were highly skilled craftsmen, and the famous bronze enamelled and engraved Birdlip Mirror is among the most prized pieces of Celtic art in Britain.

The Romans invaded the Cotswolds in AD 43, meeting little resistance from the local Dobunni tribe. They built the baths at Aqua Sulis (Bath), and Roman Corinium (Cirencester) became second only to London in size and opulence.

Corinium was the provincial capital, at the centre of a web of roads still in modern use – the Fosse Way, Ermin Street, and parts of Akeman Street. The Romans also built villas all over the Cotswolds, choosing sites carefully for their sunny aspects and water supply.

After they withdrew in AD 410, the so-called Dark Ages descended, with eventual invasion by the Saxons in AD 577. Gloucester and Winchcombe on the Wessex/Mercia border became important centres; indeed, Gloucester was vying to become the national capital.

The most obvious Saxon legacy is the very name of Cotswold itself, for it probably derives from the personal name of 'Cod', a farmer who established himself close to the source of the River Windrush near Winchcombe. The term 'Cotswold' was originally confined to this area but it has gradually encompassed more of the wolds to its present extent.

Wool had been produced in the Cotswolds since Roman times, but it came to full prominence after the Norman Conquest. By the thirteenth century, it had become immensely important to the national economy. The large local 'Cotswold lions' produced fleeces up to 2 stones (12.6 kg) in weight which, at first, were exported raw to Europe. Later, Flemish weavers helped to establish a cloth trade and, by the mid-sixteenth century, England was exporting more than 120 000 cloths per year, more than half of which were made in the Cotswolds. At the peak of the trade, there were half-a-million sheep in the Cotswolds.

Until the Industrial Revolution in the eighteenth century, the various processes of cloth production were scattered between the workers' cottages but, with the introduction of machinery such as the power loom, the clothiers gathered all production in one place. Water power was vital and the industry became concentrated alongside the more powerful streams, notably in the Stroud valleys. This area became known for its fine scarlet cloth – the 'thin red line' of the British Army. The supply from the relatively small Cotswold streams proved inadequate, however, and the area lost out to Yorkshire where the rivers are stronger. Added competition from Napoleon's Europe exacerbated the situation, and the Cotswold trade went into a decline.

There was much destitution, and it was not until the late nineteenth century that the beauty of the Cotswolds was 'discovered', largely by William Morris and his friends. He saw great virtues in the traditional architecture and skills of the area, and encouraged a whole stream of craftsmen in his wake.

Since the advent of the car, the Cotswolds have become much more widely known, and they now form a highly prized residential and tourist centre.

8 PLANTS AND ANIMALS

There are several types of landscape in the Cotswolds, each with its characteristic flora and fauna.

The wolds are good arable land but, apart from fields of growing crops, the walker may well encounter woodland, grassland, and rough grazing within the circuit of a single walk.

There are relatively few trees now on the upland, most of the woodland having been cleared by 1200. Beech is the most common species and has been called the 'wood of the oolite'. On shallower soils, ash is more predominant and oak is present on the lower slopes.

Flowers are varied and colourful. In spring, there are banks of ramsons, their white flowers like exploding cascades of fireworks. There are also bluebells, yellow archangel, wood anemone, primrose, and sweet woodruff.

Grassland is found on the highest land at the edge of the plateau, such as at Cleeve Common, with rough grazing on the steepest parts of the scarp. Depending on the level of grazing, there may be wild thyme, rock roses, vetch, cowslips, milkwort, and bird's-foot trefoil. At the sides of the roads look out for travellers' joy, scabious, toadflax, and the characteristic purple meadow cranesbill. Celandine and marsh marigold may be present in the wetter land of the valley bottoms. Some of the more unusual animals include horseshoe bats in the old quarry workings and large white edible snails in the woodland, said to have been introduced by the Romans.

Walk 1

COLN ROGERS AND WINSON

5 miles (8 km) Moderate

The Coln is one of the five main rivers which wend their way south-eastwards across the dip slope of the Cotswolds towards the Thames. It is one of the loveliest, threading between a string of beautiful villages and through the most peaceful and pastoral of landscapes. It typifies the gentle scenery of the eastern valleys.

This walk visits several of the small villages on the upper Coln. You can pass through them in minutes but they are really worthy of lengthier exploration and will often yield interesting, hidden corners or unexpected views. Also en route is a fine example of a dry valley – although it is not wholly devoid of water in winter! The walker is enfolded between its flanks which seem to exclude all sound save the bleating of the sheep.

The walk starts and finishes in Coln Rogers, a village somewhat spread out beside the river. Originally called Coln-on-the-Hill, its present name derives from Roger of Gloucester, a Norman knight. Fatally wounded in 1150, he decided for the good of his soul to grant the manor to the monks of Gloucester. The Abbot subsequently showed his gratitude for the gift by renaming the village after his benefactor.

A The church would probably be missed by the casual visitor, which may, to some extent, explain why it is comparatively less well known among Cotswold churches. It is, however, remarkable for the survival of its Saxon work – a period of history that has otherwise left very few remains. These include the original Saxon ground plan and the long and short work at the eastern and western ends of the nave. The two plaster strips and the round-headed window – cut from a single block of stone – are also typical Saxon features.

Over

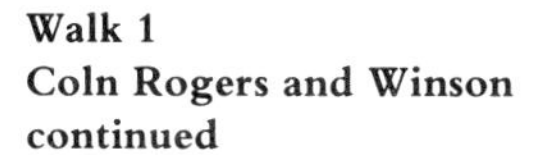

Walk 1
Coln Rogers and Winson
continued

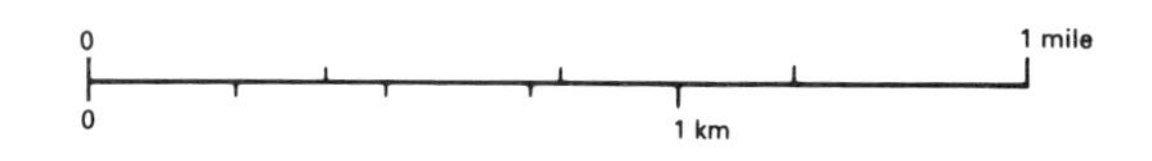

1 *Park in Coln Rogers on one of the suitably wide verges. From the bridge, take the road signposted to Winson. Bear right past the attractive thatched cottage as far as a T-junction.*

2 *Turn left into Winson and bear left at the triangular green as far as a small wicket gate on the left by a concrete footpath marker.*

3 *Turn left through the gate and cross the footbridge. Continue ahead on the path to a gate at the other side of the woodland.*

4 *Turn right before the gate to the next gate. Bear left uphill to the gate in the far corner of the field.*

5 *Continue down to the valley bottom. Turn left up the valley, cross the fence, and keep on the well-defined track until it bears sharp right.*

6 *Continue to the gate just ahead on the left in the corner. Follow the track to the road, turn left, and continue for about $\frac{3}{4}$ mile ($1\frac{1}{4}$ km) as far as Saltway Farm.*

7 *Turn left down the track in front of the farm as far as a fork by some buildings.*

8 *Take the right-hand track to the road. Turn left and go straight over at the crossroads through Calcot as far as a gate near the last house on the left.*

9 *Turn left through the gate towards the stile at the edge of the wood. Continue through the wood, cross the footbridge, and follow the track round back into the village. Access to the church is via a lane on the right just before the farmyard.*

Calcot
Upper Farm
Coln Rogers
Lower Farm
Winson
Saltway Farm
Salt Way
Lamborough Banks
Ablington Downs
River Coln

Walk 2

THE SLAUGHTERS

7½ miles (12 km) Moderate/strenuous

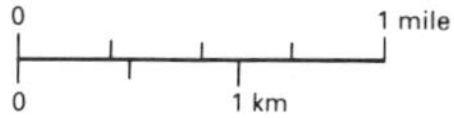

Most of this route will be unknown to the casual visitor despite the fame of the Slaughters. It explores two rivers, beginning beside the tiny River Eye, then climbing over the watershed and down into the next valley where the Windrush meanders quietly along its course.

Lower Slaughter is a renowned beauty spot with its mill, water-wheel, and post office drawing the attention of many photographers and artists. Its sister village upriver is quieter but just as

5 *Turn left for ¼ mile (400 m) to the bridleway on the right. Take the left-hand path next to the cottages and continue along the track uphill to another gate. Pass through this and continue ahead through the next two gates. Pass between the farm buildings, through a gate, and turn left on a track to the road.*

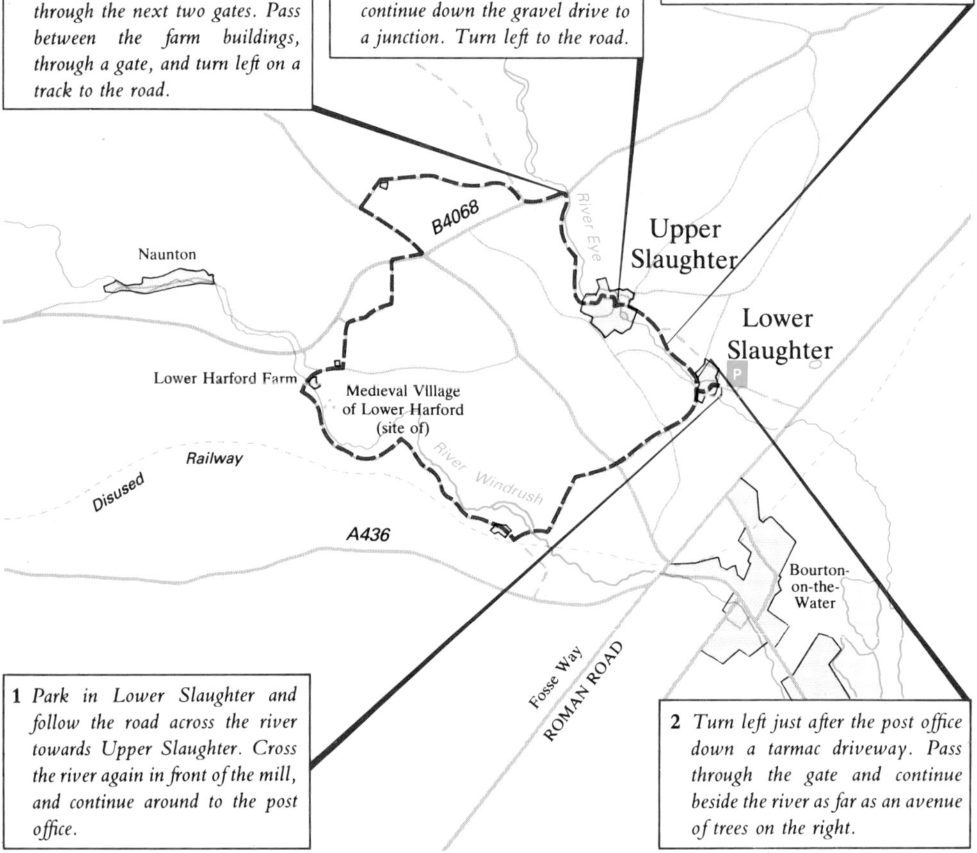

4 *Turn right and then first left by the old pump. Cross the footbridge next to the ford, then turn right back downhill to the track beside the river. Follow the track across the fields, and, at the cottage, continue down the gravel drive to a junction. Turn left to the road.*

3 *Bear half-right to a gate, then head straight across to the next gate. Continue ahead through the trees and down to the gate by the river. Cross the river and continue to the road.*

1 *Park in Lower Slaughter and follow the road across the river towards Upper Slaughter. Cross the river again in front of the mill, and continue around to the post office.*

2 *Turn left just after the post office down a tarmac driveway. Pass through the gate and continue beside the river as far as an avenue of trees on the right.*

Over

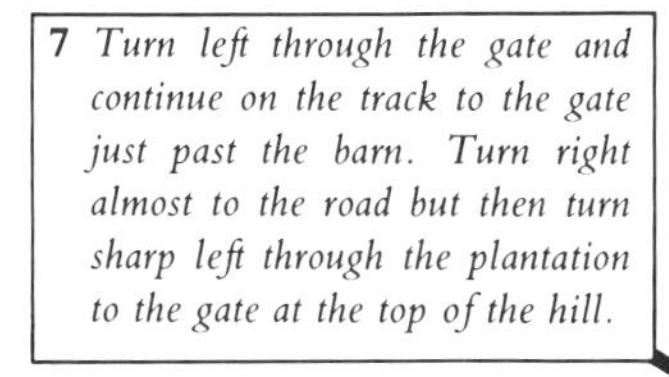

6 *Turn left to the crossroads, then turn right for about 300 yards (275 m) to a double metal bargate on the left just to the left of a wall.*

7 *Turn left through the gate and continue on the track to the gate just past the barn. Turn right almost to the road but then turn sharp left through the plantation to the gate at the top of the hill.*

8 *Walk along the left-hand edge of the field and continue through the gate by the house to the road. Turn right for about 150 yards (140 m) to a stile on the left.*

9 *Cross the stile and follow the right-hand fence to the next stile. Head downhill to the gate just to the right of the farmhouse, and on to the road.*

10 *Turn left, then bear right over the ford to a stile on the left. Cross the stile and head across the field to the next stile. Continue by the river across several stiles and gates until the path eventually bears uphill through gorse to the edge of some woodland.*

11 *Turn right along the edge of the field, go through the gate, and continue through the wood. At the open field, head towards the farm and pass through the farmyard to the road.*

12 *Turn left, cross the stream, and continue past the cottages to a gate. Turn left on to the path signposted to The Slaughters, and continue through the fields to a small bargate on the right.*

13 *Pass through the gate and cross the field to the road. Take the track opposite and, at the road junction, continue straight ahead back into Lower Slaughter.*

appealing despite, or probably because of, its less ordered appearance and layout. The former rectory – now the Lords of the Manor Hotel – was once home to the Reverend Francis Witts, a Victorian clergyman, who recorded details of daily life in this part of Gloucestershire in his famous *Diary of a Cotswold Parson*. The name of 'Slaughter' has an uncertain derivation, none as sinister as might at first be imagined. It possibly means the 'place of the sloe trees' or 'place of the pools', or may be an anglicization of the local French family name of de Sclotre.

Walk 3

NORTHLEACH AND HAMPNETT

4 miles (6½ km) Easy

The Leach is another of the larger rivers flowing south-eastwards off the wolds. This walk follows the infant river a short way close to its source at Hampnett. Like the Coln, the Leach's journey eventually ends with the merging of its waters into the Thames at Lechlade. The route then proceeds up on to the wolds before descending once more into the valley with a wonderful view of Northleach and its church.

Although the town is relatively recent – established in the early thirteenth century – the site itself is an ancient one. An Iron Age track from Chedworth crossed the Leach here and continued on to the camps at Salmonsbury (on the present site of Bourton-on-the-Water) and Maugersbury, at Stow.

The Fosse Way, just to the west of the town, was built by the Romans in about AD 60, part of a route that stretched from Exeter to Lincoln. Later still, a Saltway was established just to the south, carved by the hooves of pack horses loaded with Droitwich salt en route to London via Lechlade.

Northleach was once the centre of a large area of sheep production, and owes its existence and much of its appearance to the wool trade. It was granted a market in 1227 and, by the fourteenth century, had become the principal wool market of the central Cotswolds. The Abbey of Gloucester owned the land and planned the town around a triangular market place. Eighty plots of land were laid out along the north and south sides of the market, each 2 poles (10 m) wide and 20 yards (18 m) long – an area of about ¼ acre (0.1 ha). Many of these burgage plots have since been combined but can still be seen from high vantage points or detected in the roof lines visible from the market place.

The local wool traders became incredibly wealthy, especially those who progressed to become Merchants of the Staple. These were a group of middlemen who held the monopoly of wool export from the Crown, and traders such as the Midwinters, Forteys, and Taylors diverted part of their fortune for the construction of fine buildings including, of course, the magnificent church.

Unfortunately, the local industry was tightly controlled by the guilds who proved unable, or unwilling, to adapt to new methods of production and, after the middle of the sixteenth century, the centre of the trade shifted to Stroud. The Industrial Revolution passed by Northleach and the town has remained relatively untouched during the last two centuries.

A The parish church of Northleach is one of the three great Cotswold wool churches. There are similarities with the church at Chipping Camden that suggest the work of the same master mason. It was built on the site of a previous church and funded largely by the Fortey family.

The exterior is as notable as the beautifully light and airy interior. Of particular note is the fifteenth-century porch and stone pulpit, and the collection of famous brasses – among the finest in England.

B This used to be the prison, built in 1790 by Sir George Onesiphorus Paul. He held an interest in penal reform, and the prison was a model of its time with exercise yards, baths, and medical care. It now houses the agricultural museum but six of the cells have been reinstated. The workhouse built at the other end of town led to the saying that Northleach began in prison and ended in the workhouse.

C The interior of the church was restored in 1868 and, like it or hate it, it is certainly striking. In the eighteenth century, the rectors were notorious for marrying couples, without asking too many questions.

Over

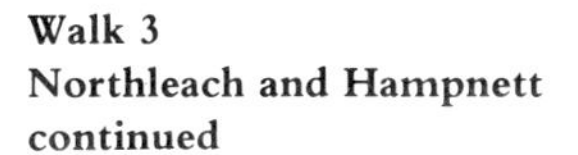

Walk 3
Northleach and Hampnett
continued

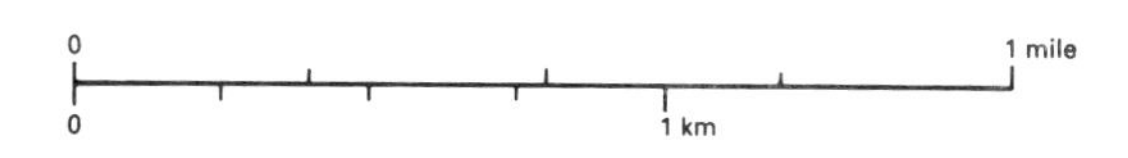

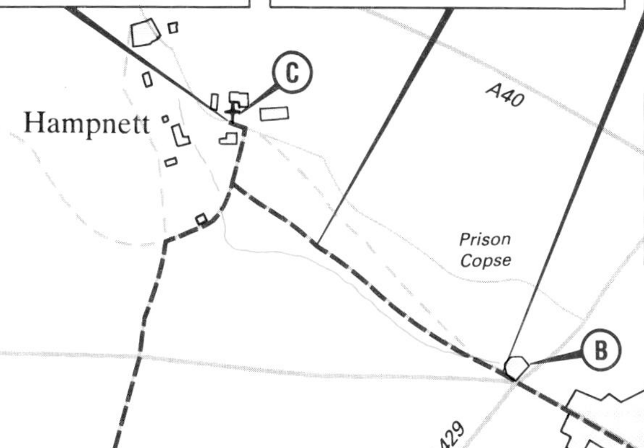

1 *Park in the town centre. Head north-westwards along the main street, and continue over the A429 to a stile on the right just past the museum.*

2 *Cross the stile and bear half-left to the corner. Cross the Leach and turn left to the gate at the end of the field. Pass through the gate, and continue straight on to the next stile.*

3 *Go over the stile and head across the field (it may be under cultivation) aiming just to the right of the big house. Cross the stile and turn right up the track to Hampnett Church.*

4 *Leave the church and return down the track. Cross the river and turn left, uphill, at the junction. Go straight on at the road and follow the right-hand field boundaries to the next road.*

5 *Turn left, go straight on at the crossroads, and, at the A429, go through the small gate opposite. Follow the left-hand field boundary on to a track, passing through farm buildings and on to a tarmac drive to the road.*

6 *Continue ahead along the left-hand dirt track as far as the last of a line of tall trees on the trackside.*

7 *Turn left through a gap in the wall and follow the left-hand field boundary downhill. Continue over a stile, heading just to the right of the church. Cross the playing field to the white gate and return to the town centre.*

Walk 4

THE LEACH VALLEY

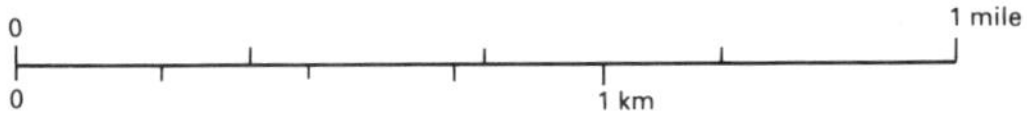

0 — 1 mile
0 — 1 km

4½ miles (7¼ km) Moderate; path through wood overgrown in places

The countryside here is quiet, offering a chance to escape the crowds and traffic. The walk follows the elusive Leach which disappears underground to emerge beneath deep, weed-covered pools, their surfaces pricked by bursting bubbles of dissolved gas.

1 *Park in Eastleach Turville and walk through the village past the church to the crossroads.*

2 *Turn left along the road to Holwell and continue past the windpump to an iron bargate on the left.*

3 *Pass through the gate and take the path through the meadows close to the river. Cross a fence and follow the river bank to the edge of the woodland ahead.*

4 *Pass through the smaller, lower gate into the wood and follow a faint path close to the wall and river on the left. Where the river bears sharp left, carry straight on and pass into a field through a gap in the wall on the right.*

5 *Follow the left-hand field boundary uphill through the woodland until the path is crossed by a well-defined track.*

6 *Turn left on to the track and continue along the left-hand edge of the fields to the road. Turn left, after walking a short way almost to the road junction.*

7 *Turn left into the field and follow the valley bottom round to a fence. Pass through the gap in the fence and follow the track to a gate by a bridge.*

8 *Pass through the gate and follow the right-hand field boundaries. At the last field before the houses, bear half-left across the field to a gate and follow the lane back into the village.*

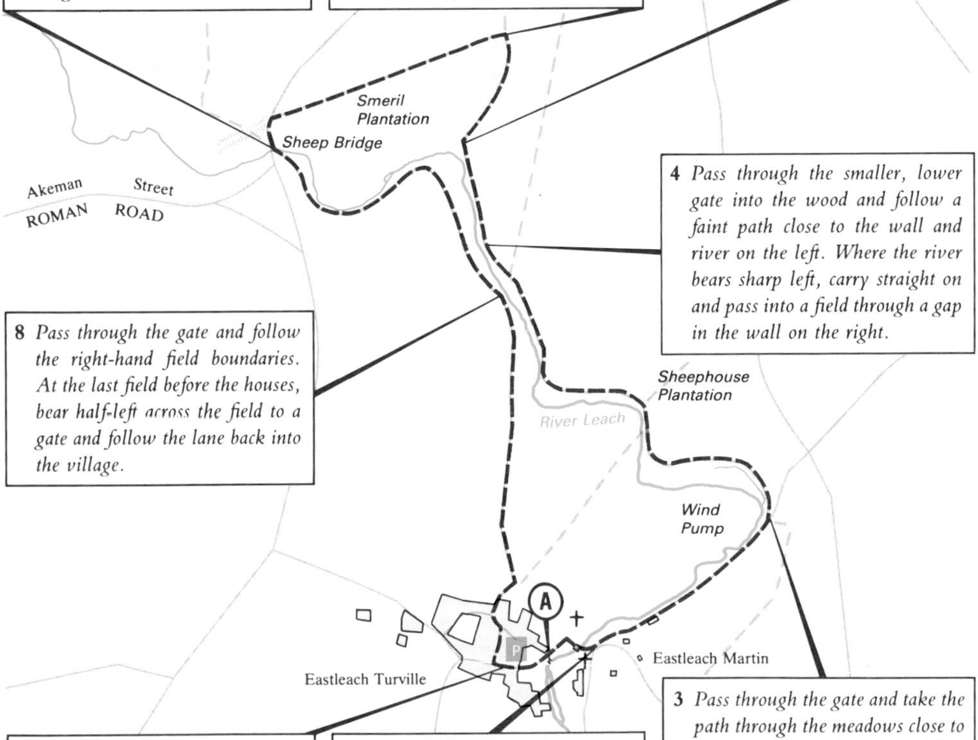

A This simple bridge is the photographic focal point of the village. It is particularly attractive in spring amid banks of daffodils. It is called Keble's Bridge after the famous local rectory who became leader of the Oxford Movement early last century.

Walk 5

CHEDWORTH WOODS

$3\frac{1}{4}$ miles ($5\frac{1}{4}$ km) Easy; one short climb, some mud

0 1 mile
0 1 km

The banks of the Coln here are clothed in very pleasant mixed woodland. In spring, the observant walker may spot the pale stalks of the parasitic toothwort or one of the large edible snails descended from those introduced by the Romans.

The walk is of a length to allow time to visit the Roman villa, regarded as one of the finest examples in Britain. The mosaics, the exposed heating systems, and the museum can easily absorb several hours.

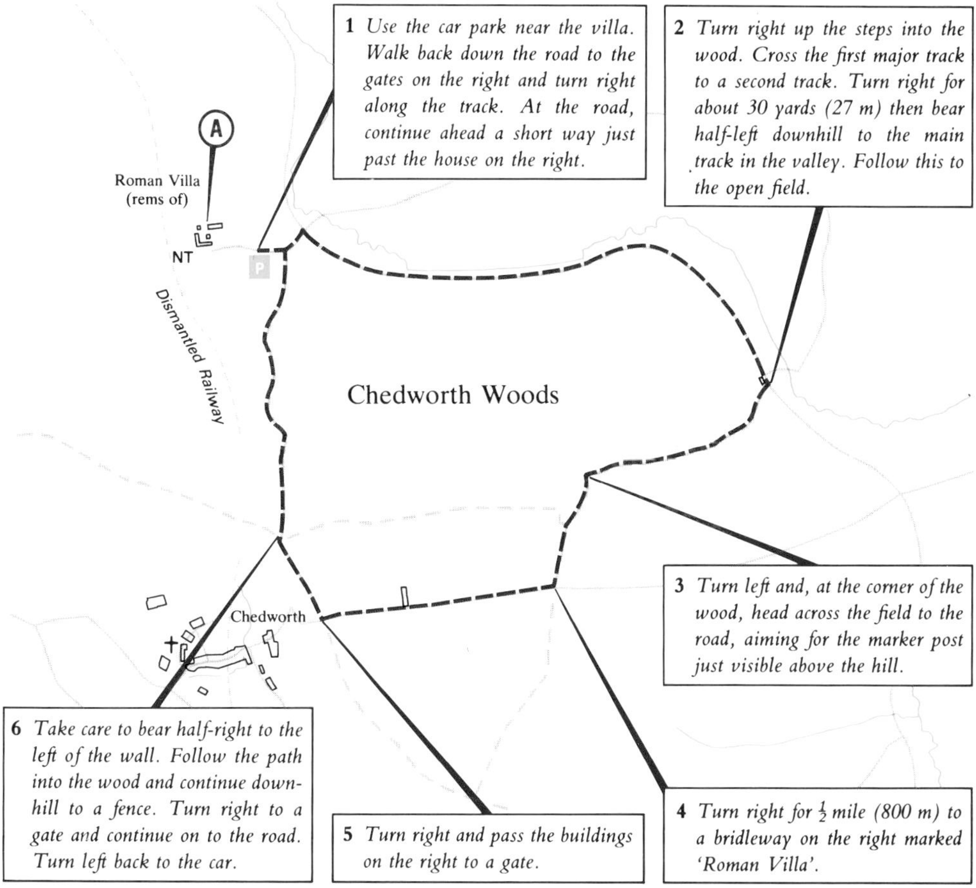

1 *Use the car park near the villa. Walk back down the road to the gates on the right and turn right along the track. At the road, continue ahead a short way just past the house on the right.*

2 *Turn right up the steps into the wood. Cross the first major track to a second track. Turn right for about 30 yards (27 m) then bear half-left downhill to the main track in the valley. Follow this to the open field.*

3 *Turn left and, at the corner of the wood, head across the field to the road, aiming for the marker post just visible above the hill.*

4 *Turn right for $\frac{1}{2}$ mile (800 m) to a bridleway on the right marked 'Roman Villa'.*

5 *Turn right and pass the buildings on the right to a gate.*

6 *Take care to bear half-right to the left of the wall. Follow the path into the wood and continue downhill to a fence. Turn right to a gate and continue on to the road. Turn left back to the car.*

A
Roman Villa
(rems of)
NT
P
Dismantled Railway
Chedworth Woods
Chedworth

A The remains were discovered by accident in 1864 by a gamekeeper who began to notice Roman debris among the rabbit burrows.

Typically, the location was chosen with care for its shelter, water supply, and communications. The first villa was built in the second century but was later altered and enlarged some time in the fourth century, from which the present buildings date. The site is thought to have been inhabited over a period of 250 years.

Walk 6

SEVEN SPRINGS AND THE DEVIL'S CHIMNEY

4¾ miles (7½ km) Easy

There is little to prepare you as you climb through the gorse of Charlton Kings Common for the extensive panorama at the top of the hill. Furthermore, as the walk progresses westwards along the edge, the view incorporates new scenery, so allow more time than usual for a walk of this length.

It is interesting to imagine how the countryside would have appeared to the Iron Age settlers who made their camp on the top of Leckhampton Hill. They enclosed a defensible area of 6 acres (2½ ha) within a single rampart and part of the scarp edge.

It soon becomes evident that the hill has been the site of intensive quarrying. It lies on the Inferior Oolite, and the freestone here occurs in outcrops up to 138 feet (42 m) thick. It was already being worked as far back as the reign of Edward III and, during the following centuries, it supplied the material used in the construction of many of Cheltenham's famous buildings.

The quarrying reached its peak during the last century and, by the late 1800s, an extensive system of tramways and railways had been constructed to transport the stone from the rock faces. Some of the inclines were incredibly steep – up to 1 in 2. The trucks were pulled by horses and proceeded down the hill and along 'The Tramroad' north to Cheltenham.

A new quarrying concern was set up in 1922 based on optimistic estimates of available yields. After a series of mishaps and local complaints, however, the company was finally wound up in 1925 and quarrying ceased on the hill.

A It used to be held that the springs issuing from this small hollow below the A436 marked the beginning of the Thames. The Latin inscription reads: *Hic Tuus – O tamesine Pater Septemgeminus fons* ('Here O father Thames is thy sevenfold source') Although the springs lie at 750 feet (228 m) – the highest point from which water flows into the Thames – it is now generally acknowledged that the river rises at Thameshead, 3 miles (5 km) south-west of Cirencester.

B There is a lot to study in this breathtaking view. Probably the first thing to catch the eye is Cheltenham spread out below the scarp. To the right you can follow the Edge as it curves around to Cleeve Hill and the highest point in the Cotswolds. Out of the plain ahead rises the graceful shape of the Malverns, composed of some of the oldest rocks in England and Wales.

Further to the west the view includes Gloucester, May Hill in the Forest of Dean, and the first of the Welsh Hills.

C This distinctive, isolated spike of rock is known as the Devil's Chimney and is a relic of the quarrying that ceased on this part of the hill around 1830.

It was originally part of a wall of rock left from the construction of a tramway in about 1800. The quarrymen gradually removed all of the wall except for this part and it became a feature of the area. It is in an unstable state and has had to be supported against the danger of collapse.

Over

Walk 6
Seven Springs and the Devil's Chimney continued

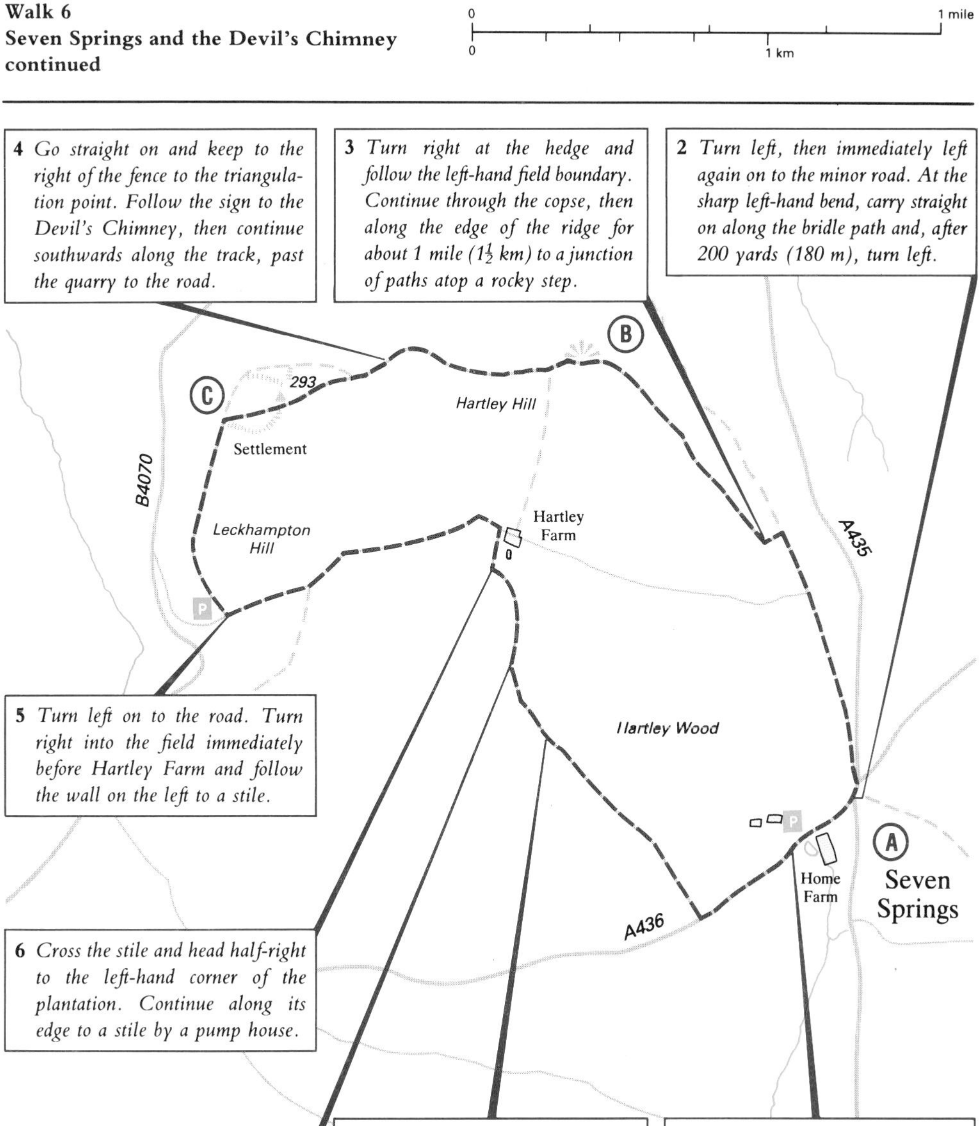

0
1 mile
0
1 km
B
C
293
Hartley Hill
Settlement
B4070
Leckhampton Hill
Hartley Farm
A435
P
Hartley Wood
P
A
Home Farm
Seven Springs
A436

1 *Park in the layby opposite The Seven Springs Inn, off the A436. Alternatively, there is parking in the old quarry at Leckhampton Hill. Turn left on to the A436 and walk to the junction.*

2 *Turn left, then immediately left again on to the minor road. At the sharp left-hand bend, carry straight on along the bridle path and, after 200 yards (180 m), turn left.*

3 *Turn right at the hedge and follow the left-hand field boundary. Continue through the copse, then along the edge of the ridge for about 1 mile (1½ km) to a junction of paths atop a rocky step.*

4 *Go straight on and keep to the right of the fence to the triangulation point. Follow the sign to the Devil's Chimney, then continue southwards along the track, past the quarry to the road.*

5 *Turn left on to the road. Turn right into the field immediately before Hartley Farm and follow the wall on the left to a stile.*

6 *Cross the stile and head half-right to the left-hand corner of the plantation. Continue along its edge to a stile by a pump house.*

7 *Cross the stile and continue ahead to the stile in the corner of the field. Cross this and follow the woodland on the left for about 200 yards (180 m).*

8 *Cross over to the woodland on the right, carrying straight on at its end and crossing a stile in the corner of the field. Carry straight on to the road and turn left to the car park.*

Walk 7

SAPPERTON AND THE GOLDEN VALLEY

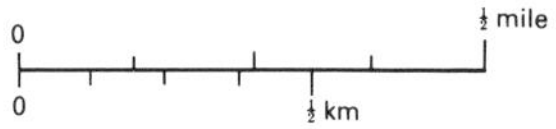

3 miles ($4\frac{3}{4}$ km) Moderate; two steep climbs, muddy

This area contains much of interest to the natural historian and to the industrial archaeologist.

Here the Thames and Severn Canal enters the Sapperton Tunnel, and the walk follows the old canal and its ruined locks to emerge into a superb piece of woodland now designated as a nature reserve.

Ferns grow in the damp tunnel entrance, and the golden heads of marsh marigolds highlight the gloomy course of the canal. The wood is best seen in spring when, among others, celandine, violets, and anemones are in flower.

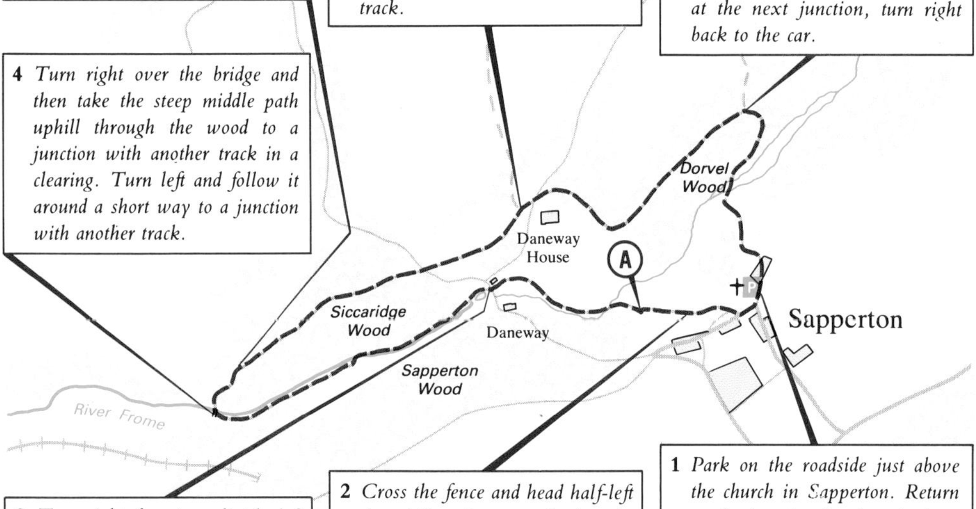

1 *Park on the roadside just above the church in Sapperton. Return to the junction by the telephone box; continue ahead and take the footpath on the right marked Daneway/Chalford. Cross the minor road and continue to a fence.*

2 *Cross the fence and head half-left downhill to the next stile (not the one in the far corner). Cross the stile and keep on this path beside the canal all the way to the road by the Daneway Inn.*

3 *Turn right then immediately left along the footpath marked 'To Chalford', eventually crossing a footbridge and reaching a brick bridge.*

4 *Turn right over the bridge and then take the steep middle path uphill through the wood to a junction with another track in a clearing. Turn left and follow it around a short way to a junction with another track.*

5 *Turn right and continue as far as the road. Go straight across and along the small valley. Head towards a house on the right when it comes into view and continue down to the road.*

6 *Turn left, then immediately right on to a track. Bear right at the fork and follow the main track through the wood, bearing left past a gate on the right and continuing as far as a crossing track.*

7 *Turn right downhill, continue over the next track, and on past the track merging from the left. Take the left fork where the track splits and continue uphill past the house to the road. Turn right and, at the next junction, turn right back to the car.*

A This is the western end of a tunnel which at 3817 yards (3481 m) long, was the longest in Britain at the time of its completion in 1789.

It is part of the Thames and Severn Canal built to connect the two rivers between Stroud and Lechlade. The boats were pushed through by men lying on their backs and walking on the tunnel roof.

The difficulty of maintaining the water level on the porous limestone, and competition from the Oxford Canal, led to its decline and abandonment early this century.

Walk 8

EDGEWORTH

0 — 1 mile
0 — 1 km

2½ miles (4 km) Easy

This upper part of the River Frome is called the Golden Valley, alluding not only to its autumn colours but also to its general beauty. Here the river's tiny proportions and secluded banks totally belie its importance and industrial setting just a few miles downstream, where it once powered the mills of the Stroud cloth industry.

This is a quiet part of the Cotswolds, and the walker may have only sheep for company. It is particularly pleasant in spring when the stream is lined with marsh marigolds and the woods are carpeted with anemones, violets, and primroses. The nearby Manor was originally built in the seventeenth century but was enlarged in the nineteenth century. It is said to occupy the site of a Roman villa.

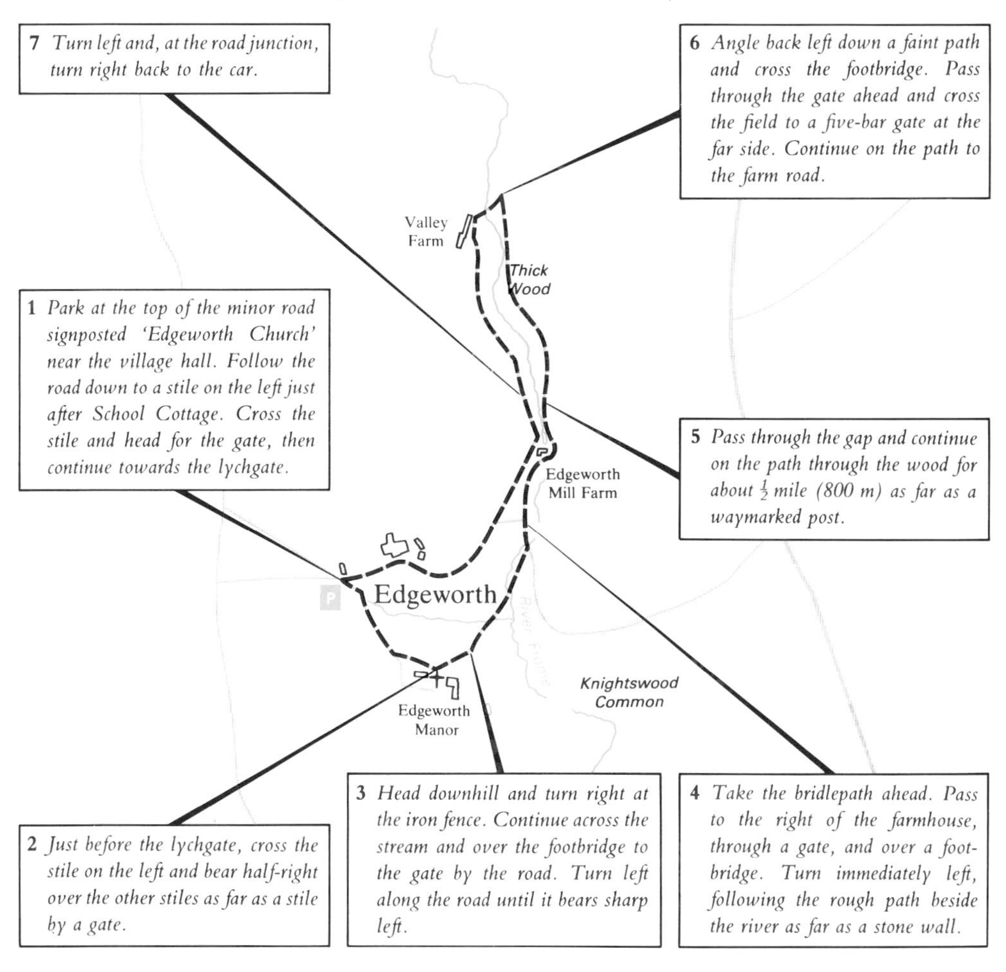

Walk 9

BIBURY AND THE COLN VALLEY

6 miles (9½ km) Moderate; some mud

This is an especially attractive section of the Coln which, here, winds its way partly through undulating parkland. The river alternately draws close then recedes from the walker among a patchwork of cropped fields and pasture. The clear water seems to be positively brimming with trout, and to sit on the banks and watch them nosing upstream is a very restful way of spending an afternoon.

Bibury is the largest and the best known of the Coln villages, its fame given an initial boost by William Morris, the Victorian artist, who described it as the most beautiful village in England. Ignoring the traffic and parked cars, you can see some justification for this, with the attractive houses, imposing mill, and lively stream burbling through the centre of it all.

In fact, the Coln separates two villages, now known collectively under the one name. Bibury lies on the east bank, with the Swan Hotel and the parish church, and Arlington lies to the west with the mill, the pub, and, of course, the famous row of cottages.

This is the modern scene but there is plenty of evidence that the area has been inhabited for over 2000 years. There is an ancient camp above Arlington, Roman remains near Bibury Court, and Saxon work in the church, some of which has been taken to the British Museum. By the time of the Norman Conquest, the village had a population of around 450 and a church of considerable size and importance.

Surprisingly, the village's first rise to fame came in the seventeenth century with the establishment of a nearby racecourse. Bibury became the headquarters of one of the oldest racing clubs in the country and, during race week, the countryside for miles around was crammed with race-goers. The attendance was no doubt boosted by the patronage of several monarchs – the meeting was particularly popular with Charles II.

The first race is thought to have been held around 1620 when plague prevented the customary meeting at Newmarket. The races were discontinued in the nineteenth century and nothing now remains of the racetrack, which was sited on the downs near Aldsworth between Burford and Bibury.

The only clue on the map lies in the local place names. 'Macaroni', for example, was the eighteenth-century nickname for the Regency dandies who patronized the racing, and it is thought that the grandstand stood near Macaroni Downs Farm.

A There were many mills on the Coln and, at the time of the Domesday survey in 1086, there were five in Bibury alone.

This site was one of those recorded, and the mill here has been used for both wool and corn. It was rebuilt in the eighteenth century and strengthened in 1850, but has since been converted into an interesting museum of country crafts.

B Arlington Row could be the blueprint for the traditional English cottage. It is now in the hands of the National Trust but was originally a fourteenth-century wool store, later converted into weavers' cottages.

In front of the row, and surrounded by water, lies the Rack Isle where the weavers hung their woollen cloth on oak racks to dry after fulling.

C The route here crosses the line of Akeman Street, a Roman road that stretched from Exeter to Cirencester. It is difficult to make out at this point, especially when we consider that the Romans built their roads to a standard width of 84 feet (25½ m). Akeman Street was once part of the coach route to London. Just over a mile (1½ km) to the west lies the curiously named Ready Token, once a coaching inn where no credit was available, its services having to be paid for in cash.

Over

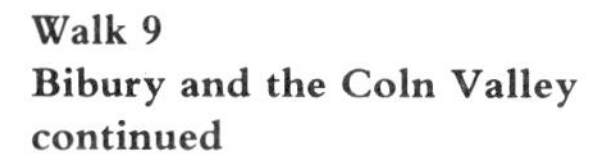

Walk 9
Bibury and the Coln Valley continued

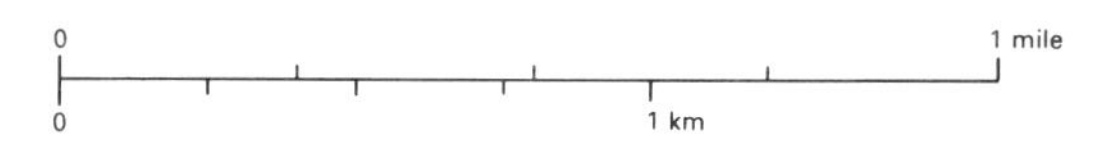

1 *Park in Bibury either in front of the museum or beside the river. Walk south down the main road and cross the last footbridge opposite the craft shop. Go past Arlington Row and continue up the hill.*

2 *At the small green, turn left towards Ready Token and pass through the iron gate. Continue through the next gate and then along the right-hand edge of the fields as far as another iron gate.*

3 *Turn left before the gate on to a grassy track and follow this for about 1 mile (1½ km) to the road. Turn left.*

4 *Turn left again on to the bridleway just past Coneygar Lodge. Head towards the house just to the left of the farm buildings. Go through the gate and continue to the next gate to the right of the house.*

5 *Head across the field towards the gap in the wall and continue on the path across the field to the gate.*

6 *Pass through the gate and walk along the right-hand edge of the field. Where the wall ends, bear left downhill among the beech trees and cross the stile. Turn left at the river and cross the meadow to the gate at the far end.*

7 *Pass through the wood and follow the track through the fields by the river, eventually reaching an iron gate at the edge of Ash Copse.*

8 *Walk straight on to the gate ahead, across the fields to a stile, and follow the path uphill, continuing to a junction of tracks.*

9 *Turn right downhill and follow the track through the buildings, past the hotel, and on up to the road. Turn left and then left again back into Bibury.*

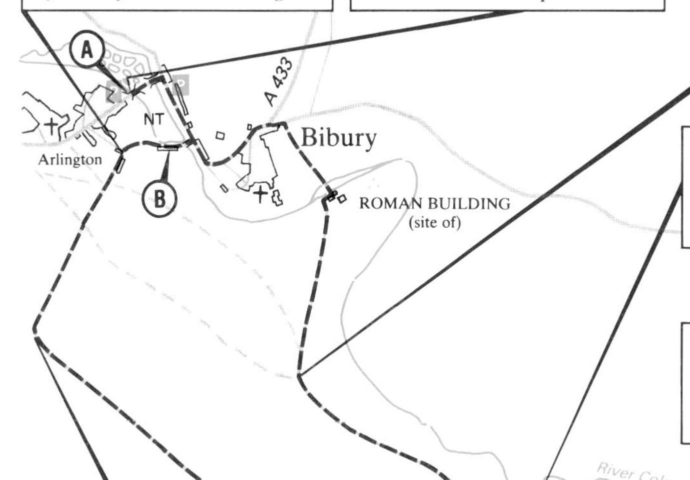

Walk 10

UPPER SLAD VALLEY

5¾ miles (9¼ km) Strenuous; some mud, path steep in places

The Slad valley was once one of the most important mill valleys in the Cotswolds. Today it is quiet and relatively unspoilt. This is a fairly demanding route with ascents and descents between several small, remote valleys. The walker is rewarded, however, with good views over Painswick and the Dillay valley, beautiful woodland and secluded, intimate countryside.

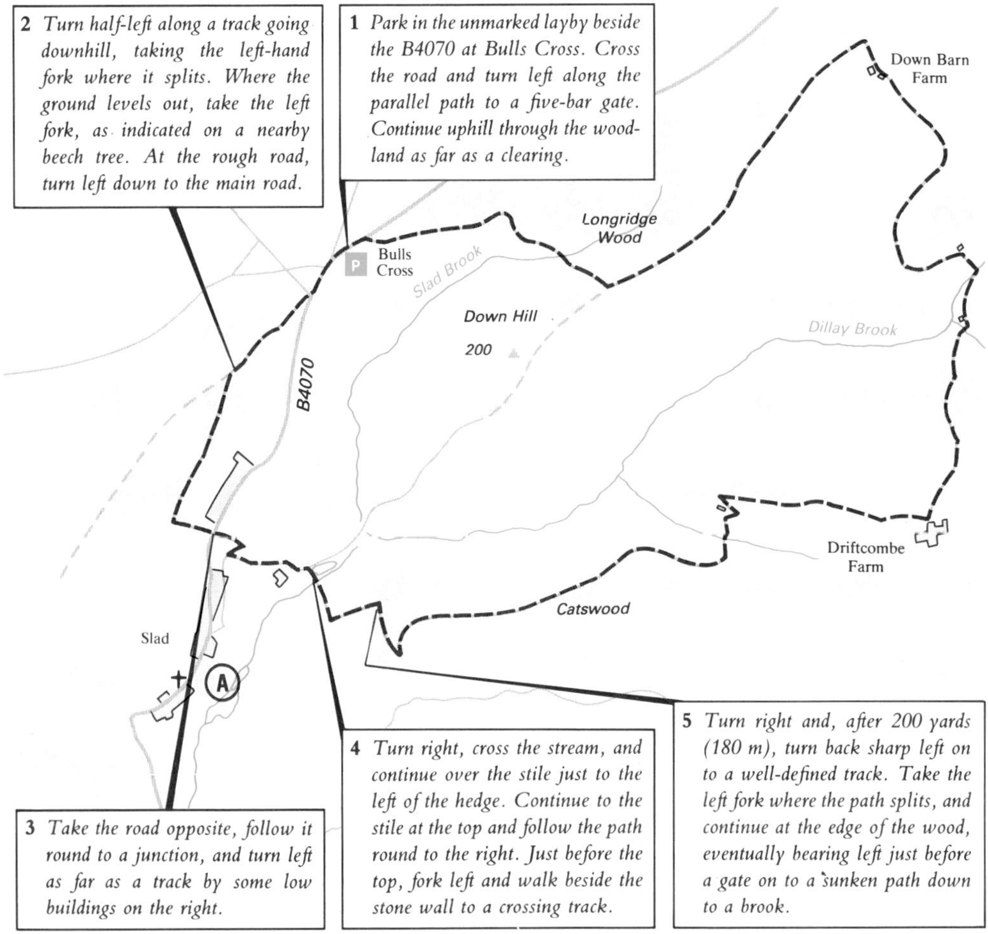

1 *Park in the unmarked layby beside the B4070 at Bulls Cross. Cross the road and turn left along the parallel path to a five-bar gate. Continue uphill through the woodland as far as a clearing.*

2 *Turn half-left along a track going downhill, taking the left-hand fork where it splits. Where the ground levels out, take the left fork, as indicated on a nearby beech tree. At the rough road, turn left down to the main road.*

3 *Take the road opposite, follow it round to a junction, and turn left as far as a track by some low buildings on the right.*

4 *Turn right, cross the stream, and continue over the stile just to the left of the hedge. Continue to the stile at the top and follow the path round to the right. Just before the top, fork left and walk beside the stone wall to a crossing track.*

5 *Turn right and, after 200 yards (180 m), turn back sharp left on to a well-defined track. Take the left fork where the path splits, and continue at the edge of the wood, eventually bearing left just before a gate on to a sunken path down to a brook.*

A This small village is known the world over for its association with the author, Laurie Lee. He grew up in Slad and still lives in the village.

His most famous work, *Cider With Rosie,* is set in the valley at a time of relative isolation before the advent of modern communications.

This is a world long since disappeared, but it is still possible to

Over

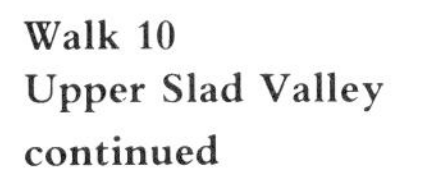

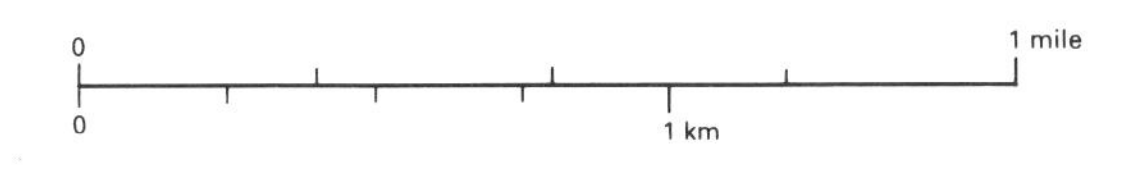

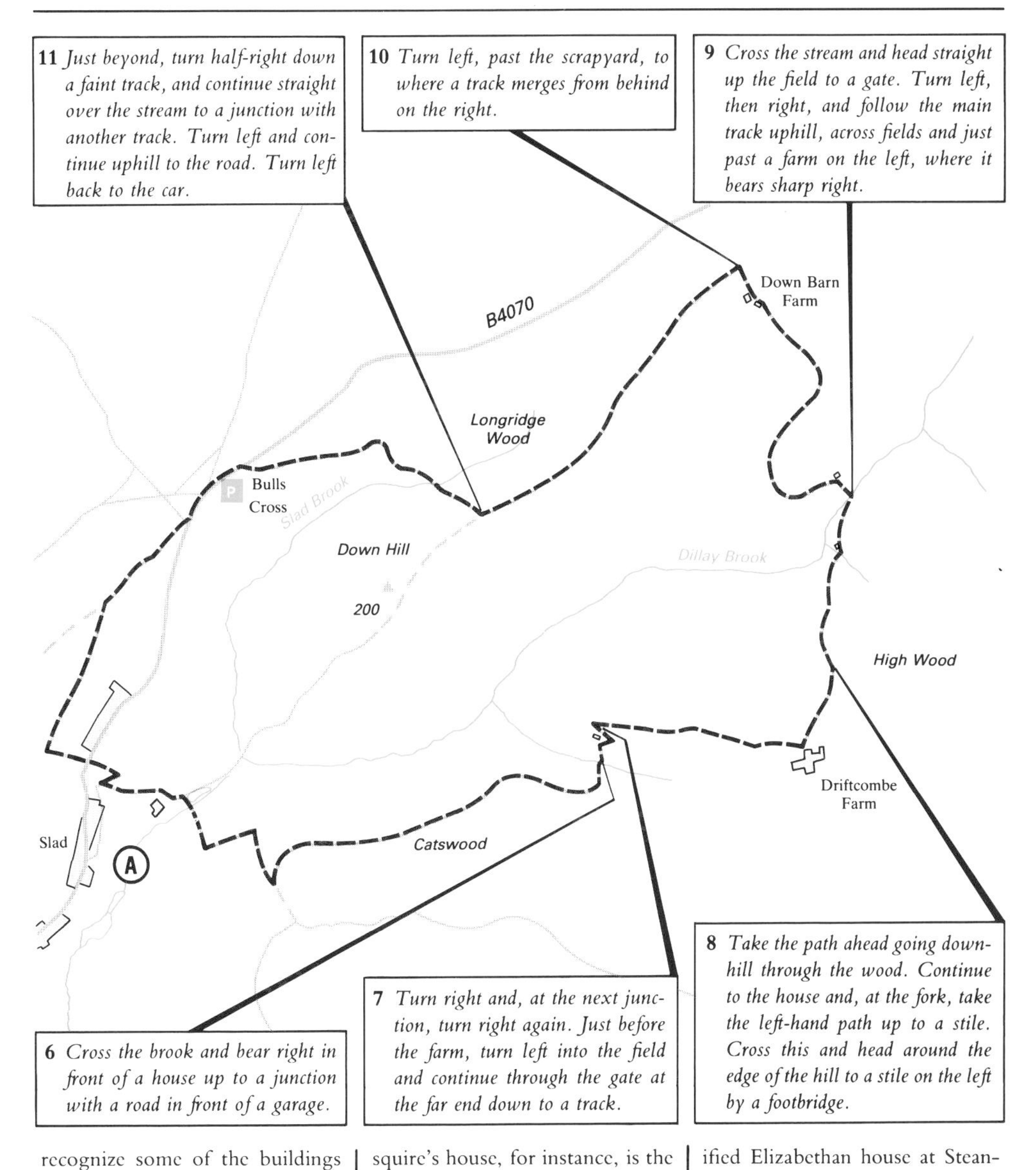

recognize some of the buildings mentioned in the book. The squire's house, for instance, is the literary counterpart for the modified Elizabethan house at Steanbridge, down by the brook.

Walk 11

LONG COMPTON AND THE ROLLRIGHT STONES

$6\frac{3}{4}$ miles ($10\frac{3}{4}$ km) Moderate; some mud

Here in the northern Cotswolds, the valleys open out and the scenery rolls gently into the distance. This can be seen near the top of the valley where there is a fine view to the north and west.

The road at the top separates Oxfordshire from Warwickshire and lies on the site of an ancient track that ran along the high ground from Edge Hill to Bath. Prehistory is evident again within the mysterious circle of the Rollright Stones.

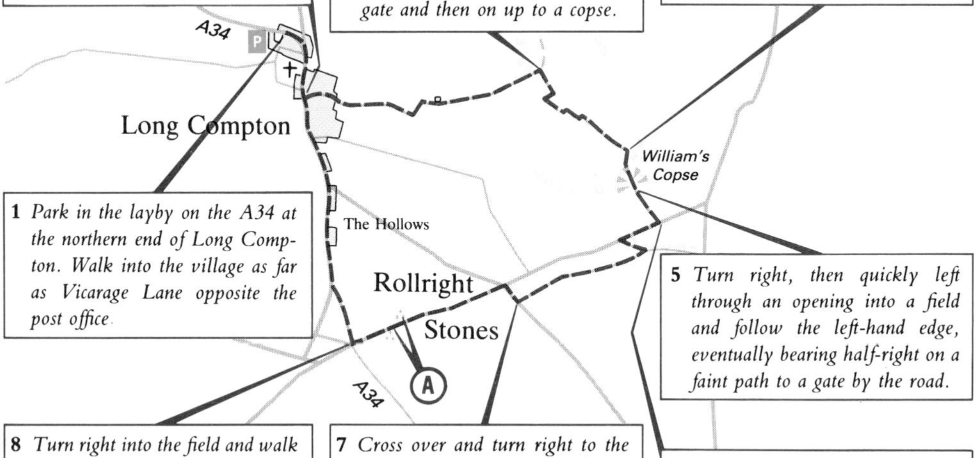

1 *Park in the layby on the A34 at the northern end of Long Compton. Walk into the village as far as Vicarage Lane opposite the post office.*

2 *Turn left and carry straight on where the road turns sharp right. Continue along the track for about a mile ($1\frac{1}{2}$ km) through gates and fields until it turns left uphill to a house.*

3 *Turn right through the opening down the right-hand edge of the field. Cross the footbridge and enter the field. Turn right and, at the hedge, turn left, following the right-hand edge of the field to a gate and then on up to a copse.*

4 *Turn right through the gate, following the left-hand field boundary to the corner. Go through the right-hand gate and along the left-hand edge of the field to the next gate.*

5 *Turn right, then quickly left through an opening into a field and follow the left-hand edge, eventually bearing half-right on a faint path to a gate by the road.*

6 *Turn right and, at the next junction, turn left. After about 250 yards (230 m), turn right through a gate and continue along the track, then through the fields beside the hedge. Continue straight ahead down the steps to the road.*

7 *Cross over and turn right to the crossroads. Turn left for $\frac{1}{2}$ mile (800 m) to a stile on the right near the King's Stone. Return to the road and, after 50 yards (45 m), turn left to the stone circle. Return to the road and turn left as far as the junction.*

8 *Turn right into the field and walk towards the end of the distant hedge ahead. Continue to the left of this down to the road. Turn right, then turn left on the A34 back into the village.*

A About seventy-six stones make up the circle known as the Kings Men and were long believed to possess special powers.

In legend, they represent the silent army of an ambitious nobleman. He was tempted by a witch with the Crown of England if he could sight Long Compton within seven strides, and failing to do so, was turned into stone along with his knights, who form the circle and a small group to the east known as the Whispering Knights. The King Stone stands alone and, paradoxically, soldiers would take chippings as good luck charms. The Circle was built around 2000 BC and is probably a religious site associated with sun worship.

Walk 12
BROADWAY

0 — 1 mile
0 — 1 km

3½ miles (5½ km) Moderate; one long climb, some mud

Broadway is named after the width of the main street, dictated by two streams running either side. These are now covered, but the wonderful architecture remains to view.

Broadway originally prospered from its position on the London to Worcester coach route and, at one time, there were more than twenty inns. As at Bibury, William Morris popularized the village.

1 *Use the car park off the B4632 Stratford road. Walk east down the main A44 as far as a footpath on the left marked 'Chipping Camden' just after Pike Cottage.*

2 *Turn left and follow the railings. Continue over a stile, then through a gate and to the left of the hedge. Follow the left-hand edge of the next field and continue following the waymarks uphill to the road.*

3 *Take the path opposite to where it splits near the top. Turn right, and at the next junction, turn left following the sign to 'Fish Hill'. Eventually, bear left and climb up the steps to the road.*

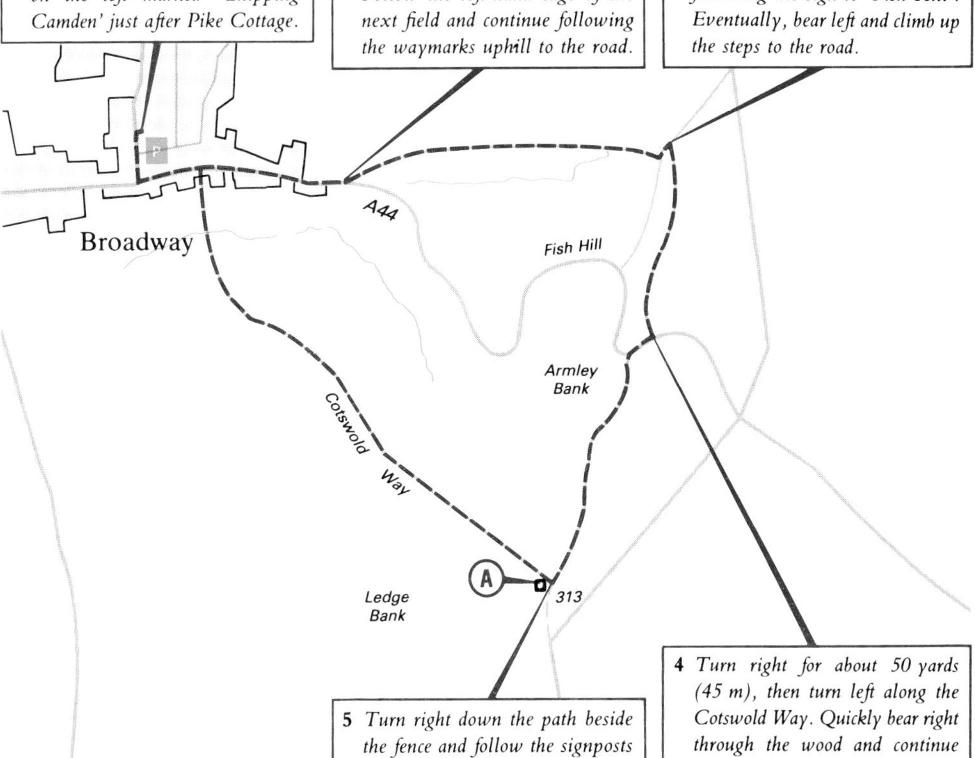

5 *Turn right down the path beside the fence and follow the signposts back into Broadway.*

4 *Turn right for about 50 yards (45 m), then turn left along the Cotswold Way. Quickly bear right through the wood and continue along the grassy path to the Tower.*

A The Tower occupies the second highest point of the Cotswolds at 1024 feet (312 m). The extensive view covers twelve counties and includes the Black Mountains, the Malverns, the Clee Hills, and the Wrekin.

It was designed by James Wyatt and built in 1799 by the Earl of Coventry for his wife. It is constructed from a dark, non-native stone and remained in private hands until 1972, since when it has formed the centrepiece for a country park.

Walk 13

WINCHCOMBE AND SUDELEY CASTLE

0 1 mile
0 1 km

5 miles (8 km) Moderate; two climbs

Allow plenty of time for this walk to take in the views, perhaps visit the castle, and to wander around Winchcombe, an interesting old town full of character.

Winchcombe nestles below the Edge beside the River Isbourne, an important site with a long history. It rose to prominence as a Saxon town, when it became a provincial capital of Mercia.

1 *There is a car park in the town. Walk back to the main A46 road and turn left for ⅓ mile (500 m) to Rushley Lane on the right.*

2 *Turn right into Rushley Lane and, at the bend, continue ahead down Stancombe Lane to a stile on the left near a shed.*

3 *Bear half-left to the gap in the fence and follow the waymarks uphill. Continue beside the wood on the right up to a fence at the top. Turn left to a stile.*

4 *Cross the stile and walk down the left side of the field to an old wall. Bear slightly right, cross the stile, and continue to the top. Turn left and, at the stone wall, turn left again and continue down to a stile.*

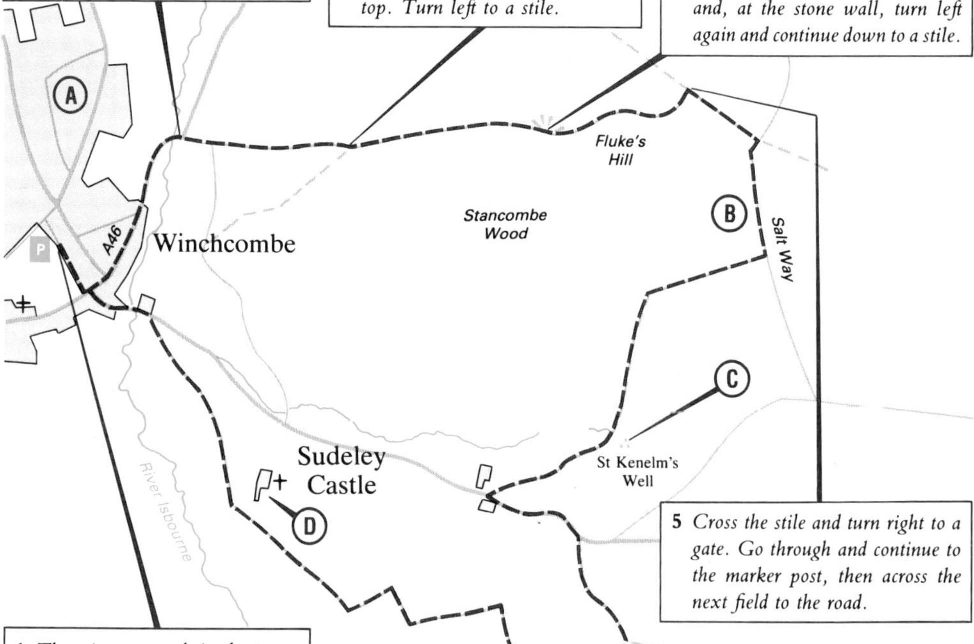

5 *Cross the stile and turn right to a gate. Go through and continue to the marker post, then across the next field to the road.*

A The town grew up around the Abbey which was founded in AD 798 and became one of the largest landowners in the Cotswolds.

The Abbey was dissolved in 1539 and nothing now remains.

The church has a splendid weathercock and an interesting collection of forty gargoyles known as the 'Winchcombe Worthies'.

B This ancient route originated at Droitwich, where the salt was especially pure, and passed through the Cotswolds to London via Lechlade and the Thames.

Over

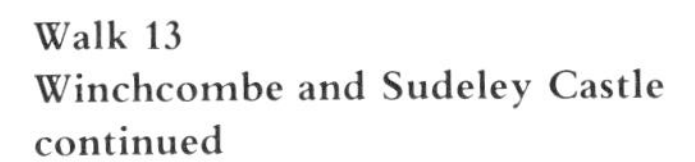

Walk 13
Winchcombe and Sudeley Castle continued

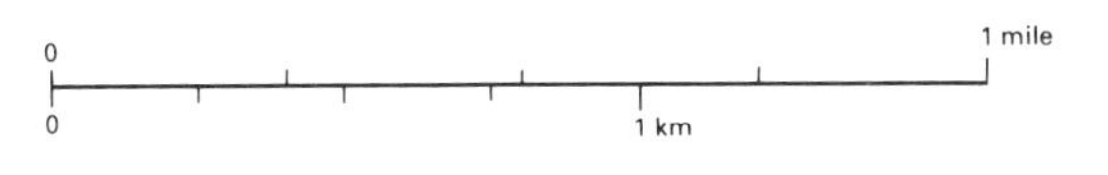

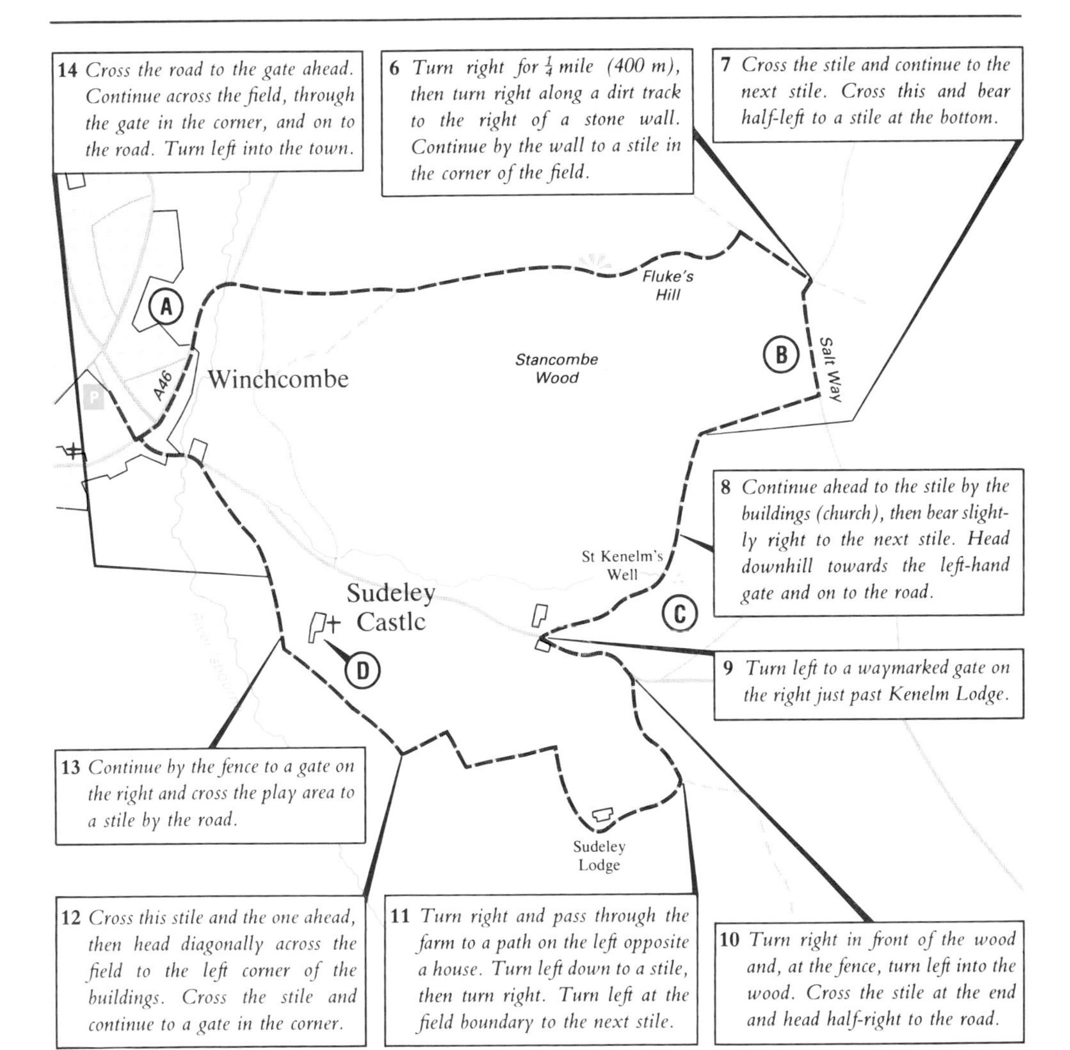

C This spring is said to mark the final halt of the body of Kenelm before it reached Winchcombe.

He became King of Mercia as a young boy but was murdered at the instigation of his jealous sister in AD 819. The monks at Winchcombe recovered his body and springs gushed out wherever they laid him. The well became a shrine for many pilgrims.

D The castle was home to Katherine Parr, the sixth wife of Henry VIII. It was slighted after the Civil War, and even became an inn before restoration in the nineteenth century.

Walk 14

CLEEVE COMMON AND BELAS KNAP

8 miles (13 km) Some exposed high ground, best left for a clear day, compass useful

Cleeve Common is the largest expanse of unenclosed land left in the Cotswolds and virtually the only area approaching the nature of an upland. This route is best tackled in good conditions, not only to appreciate the superb view, but also because the visibility may be quickly reduced to a few yards in low cloud. The common can resemble bleak moorland in these instances but, otherwise, any sense of isolation is modified somewhat by the golf course, the car parks, and the radio masts.

The highest point in the Cotswolds lies at 1083 feet (329 m) just a few hundred yards to the south-east of the masts, marked by a triangulation pillar.

The short, springy turf provides a pleasant surface underfoot but is now confined to a few sites on the highest parts of the edge, as at Charlton Kings Common, Minchinhampton, Haresfield Beacon, and Painswick Hill.

The golf course occupies a fair chunk of the western part of the common and, for the most part, flying golf balls pose the biggest threat to the walker. The golf club, of course, is quite modern but some of its greens are of considerably greater vintage. One of them lies within the defences of an Iron Age hillfort, and yet another occupies an ancient 30-yard (27-m) wide circular enclosure known as 'The Ring'. This feature is not yet fully understood but is possibly the site of some religious ritual.

At the edge of the escarpment, and just off the route, lies an expanse of bare rock known as 'Cleeve Cloud' from the Anglo-Saxon 'clif', a cliff, and 'clud', a rock mass and from which the common derives its name.

A Belas Knap is one of the hundred or so Neolithic long barrows found in the Cotswold region, constructed some time around 3500 BC, and part of the distinctive Severn-Cotswold series of chambered tombs. It belongs to the second and later phase of construction with a false portal and chambers entered from the side. They were built of local stone and surrounded by a retaining wall, the whole being turfed over to form a mound which originally probably extended to 200 feet by 80 feet (60 x 24 m). The monument now measures about 180 feet by 60 feet (55 x 24 m) and up to 13 feet (4 m) at its highest point.

The function of the curved horns at the false entrance are not entirely understood but may have been significant for the rituals of interment.

The presence of Roman coins suggests that there has been interest in the site for a very long time. The major excavations occurred in 1863–65 and 1928–30 during which the remains of over thirty individuals and various animals were found.

Unfortunately, the nineteenth-century work damaged the original portal lintel which had to be replaced, and the original stonework had to be replaced or rebuilt elsewhere. The lower courses of the horns are, however, as the Neolithic builders laid them, and their similarity to modern dry stone walling shows that the method of construction has remained unaltered for over 5000 years.

B The Domesday survey records the presence of mills here using the water of the Isbourne to grind corn. From late Tudor times onward, an increasing number of mills was converted to the manufacture of paper, beginning in the Cotswolds at Stanway in the mid-seventeenth century. These mills did not start paper making until the early eighteenth century, taking advantage of the purity of the water supply to make coloured papers. Today, the mills are major producers of high-quality filter paper for use in industry, hospital, and laboratory work.

Most of the architecture is relatively modern but there are a few remaining parts of the eighteenth- and nineteenth-century buildings.

Over

Walk 14
Cleeve Common and Belas Knap continued

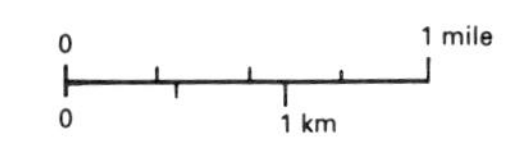

1 *Park in one of the laybys off the A46 at Cleeve Hill. Take the path opposite the telephone box straight up on to the common to a marker post.*

2 *Turn right, then soon bear left towards the top of the hill. Take one of the paths heading towards the radio masts.*

3 *From the radio masts, head east (half-right with back to the fence) across the common, towards a clump of gorse. After about ¼ mile (400 m) bear half-right (south-east) to a grassy track to a gate at the edge of the common.*

4 *Go through the gate and follow the track, turning left at the farm buildings, and eventually turning right on to the footpath to Belas Knap.*

5 *Cross the stile, turn left, and go through the kissing gate. Follow the right-hand field boundaries, turning left at the end of the second field, then right through the kissing gate down to the road.*

6 *Turn left and, at the junction, take the footpath to Postlip. Bear left towards the corner of the field and a track.*

7 *Cross the track and follow the grassy track skirting to the left of the pond, continuing beside the fence on the right to a stile in the corner.*

8 *Cross the stile and follow the faint track around the hillside. Cross the stile and follow the right-hand field boundary downhill. Continue through the farm and go straight on at the junction to the mill complex.*

9 *Follow the drive uphill, then turn left on the drive through the mill to a gate at the end of the car park. Go straight on where the track bears left through a gate and cross the footbridge on the left into the field. Follow the right-hand field boundaries to a drive.*

10 *Go straight over and keep to the left of the wall to a gate. Turn right and pass through the farm. At the corner of the wall, turn left through a gate, then straight on through another gate to the edge of the common.*

11 *Turn right along the edge of the woodland to a road. Turn sharp left and pass through a gate on the right after 200 yards (180 m). Follow the track back to the common and continue along its edge back to the car.*

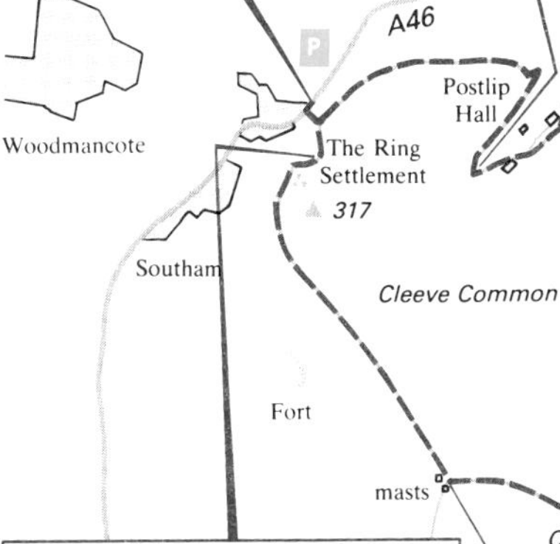

Walk 15

BURFORD AND WIDFORD

5¾ miles (9¼ km) Moderate; some mud

There is a contrast on this walk between an often busy town and quiet riverside scenery.

Lying on their eastern edge, Burford is often called 'Gateway to the Cotswolds', and its position on the London to Gloucester coach road was instrumental in its growth.

It is an attractive and historic town, and well worth a diversion to explore its side roads and shops. This can be done at either end of the walk, although a cup of tea and cream cake on the way around the town seems a very satisfactory way to round off the day's exertions.

A The Romans chose to cross the Windrush a little further downstream, and routed Akeman Street through Asthall. The Saxons did settle here, however, and the ford became important as a route between Wessex and Mercia. The town's location was certainly important to its growth, but there were other factors that were to ensure its prosperity over the succeeding centuries.

The surrounding area was good sheep land and, by the sixteenth century, there was a thriving cloth industry. As elsewhere, the appearance of the town benefited from the wealth of the wool merchants who paid for buildings such as Falkland Hall in the High Street, constructed for Edmund Sylvester the clothier in 1558.

The church also benefited enormously, of course, and it was almost continually altered over several centuries from an original long, low, barn-like structure in the twelfth century to the magnificent building seen today. Externally, all the major periods of religious architecture are represented up to about 1500, after which the building stopped with the gradual decline in the wool trade.

Inside, there is a pagan carving of three figures dated AD 100, and the lead lining of the fourteenth-century font is inscribed with the signature of Anthony Sedley, one of the Levellers who mutinied against Cromwell in 1649 in anger at their lack of pay and Cromwell's undemocratic rule. They marched from Salisbury to Burford where they were captured by Cromwell and held in the church. Three of them were shot in the churchyard and the others made to watch.

Wool was not the only commodity that underpinned the wealth of the town, for just upstream lies a series of quarries that has produced some of the finest stone in the Cotswolds. There have been quarries at Taynton for over 900 years, and the honey-coloured stone of this quarry in particular is famous for its quality. It was used by Wren for the dome of St Paul's Cathedral, by Vanbrugh for the building of Blenheim Palace, in many of the Oxford colleges, and in St George's Chapel, Windsor.

Other historic buildings in the town include a row of almshouses near the church built in 1457 by the Earl of Warwick. There is an informative town guide available from the Tourist Information Centre.

B The church of St Oswald now stands curiously isolated but, in 1381, there were thirteen households nearby comprising Old Widford. The village was presumably decimated by the Black Death and, by 1524, there were just three households recorded. The church was built by the monks of Gloucester, and possibly stands on the site where the body of St Oswald rested on its way to Gloucester from Lindisfarne after his death in AD 642.

There is much of interest inside. The original Saxon church was rebuilt around 1100 on the floor of a Roman villa, and a section of the tessellated pavement has been exposed. This was discovered, along with the fourteenth-century murals, during restoration work in 1904 after a forty-year period of disuse.

Over

Walk 15
Burford and Widford
continued

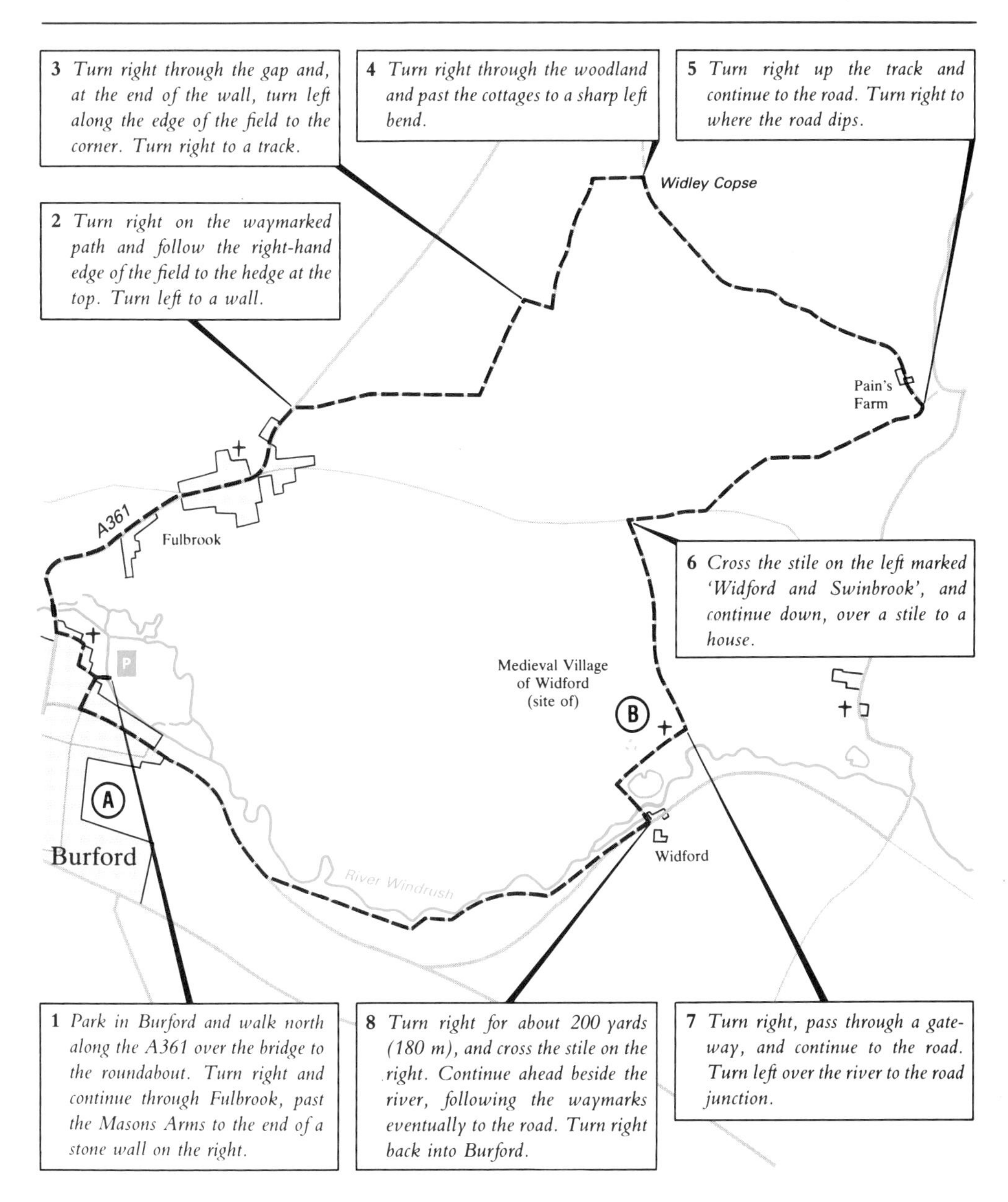

Walk 16

STANTON AND STANWAY

$4\frac{3}{4}$ miles ($7\frac{1}{2}$ km) Moderate; one long climb, some mud

A large section of this walk follows the well-signposted Cotswold Way, visiting two beautiful villages at the foot of the escarpment.

The route climbs over the rough grazing land above Stanton to the top of the Edge – favoured as a defensive site in the Iron Age – and returns down through some beautiful mixed woodland to Stanway. The last mile or so passes through attractive parkland and fields to Stanton, one of the least spoilt villages in the Cotswolds.

A Stanton was one of the first conserved villages and owes much of its restoration to the architect, Sir Philip Stott, who bought the estate in 1906. He spent thirty years restoring the village and, after his death, the council continued in the same manner by constructing houses in the traditional style.

The single street heading east from the church is especially notable and, because it peters out into a track, it has the further virtue of being unmarred by through traffic.

The houses were constructed between the late sixteenth and mid-seventeenth centuries, some having their dates carved into the lintels – 1604, 1615, 1618. They display all the classic features of the Cotswold style with their drip moulds, stone mullions, and dormer windows.

The church is twelfth to fifteenth century and has strong links with John Wesley who, at one time, preached regularly from Stanton and the surrounding area. Inside there is a rare fourteenth-century wooden pulpit, and the pew ends bear gouge marks made by the ropes attached to the shepherds' dogs.

B The hill fort at Shenberrow lies at over 900 feet (275 m) and commands a good view over the vale. It was built during the Iron Age some time between 700–150 BC although, being of bivallate (double ramparts) structure, it probably dates from the later end of the period.

It originally covered about 3 acres (1¼ ha), and is one of about seventeen hill forts located on the edge of the escarpment. Unfortunately, though, it has suffered much destruction and is not one of the best examples.

C Stanway House is a fine Jacobean building built by Sir Paul Tracy early in the seventeenth century. Interestingly, it was one of the last residences to be built with a great hall where the owner and his family dined with the servants.

Extensive modifications made in the nineteenth and twentieth centuries were removed in 1948, and much of the present building is original. The massive south gate facing the road seems over-elaborate by comparison, and was built by Timothy Strong of Taynton after the style of Inigo Jones.

The occupants of the house include Dr Thomas Dover, grandson of the inventor of the Olympick Games held above Chipping Camden. He was known for his mercury-based medicines but is chiefly remembered as the rescuer of Alexander Selkirk from the island of Juan Fernandez in 1708. The latter gentleman is better known for his literary identity as Robinson Crusoe.

D This rather unusual cricket pavilion was given to the village by Sir James Barrie, one-time owner of Stanway House. The thatched building rests on staddle stones, a characteristic feature of Cotswold barns.

Over

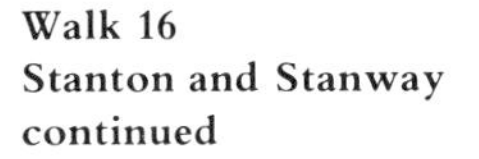

Walk 16
Stanton and Stanway
continued

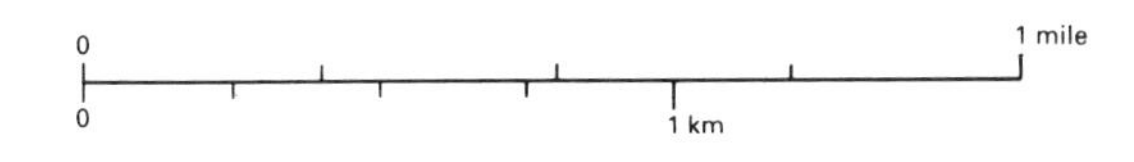

1 *Use the car park next to the cricket pitch in Stanton. Turn right out of the car park and, at the junction, turn left as far as the fork near Pear Tree Cottage.*

2 *Turn right and follow the sign to Shenberrow Hill (the route is waymarked). Continue on the track and turn right just before a gate down to a stile. Cross this and continue to the next stile.*

3 *Bear half-right to a stile. Cross this and follow the wall on the left to the next stile. Cross over and head half-right. At the junction with the path, turn right and continue uphill to a gate beside the farm.*

4 *Continue ahead to a signpost on the right and turn right, passing through the farm to a gate. Continue along the right-hand edge of the field to the next gate, then bear half-left to a stile.*

5 *Turn left and enter the wood. At the junction with the track, turn right and follow the bridleway into the wood, following the marker posts to the road.*

6 *Turn right and continue along the main road to a stile on the right marked 'Stanton'. Follow the path to the road and turn right past Stanway House (and the unusual cricket pavilion) to a stile on the right.*

7 *Cross the stile and follow the waymarks through the parkland and the fields to a stile before the buildings. Turn left to the road and then turn right. At the junction turn left back to the car.*

A
Stanton
P
Settlement
B
Shenberrow Hill
290
Cotswold Way
Lidcombe Hill
Lidcombe Wood
D
C
Stanway House
Stanway
B4077

Walk 17

SNOWSHILL

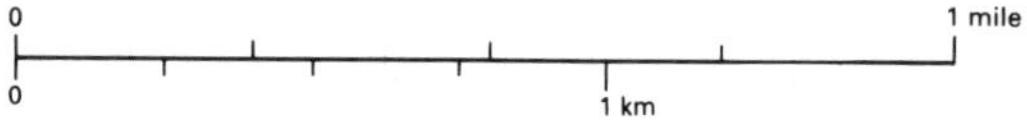

2¼ miles (3½ km) Easy; one long climb

This is a good walk for a peaceful afternoon stroll. Snowshill itself is a small village, its picturesque cottages clustered around the sloping green. At 750 feet (229 m), it lies high up on the wolds and has a remote airy feel.

Near the end of the walk, the route passes through a small, secluded copse that, in early summer, is carpeted with yellow archangel and horsetails among others. The final climb offers good views back over the valley.

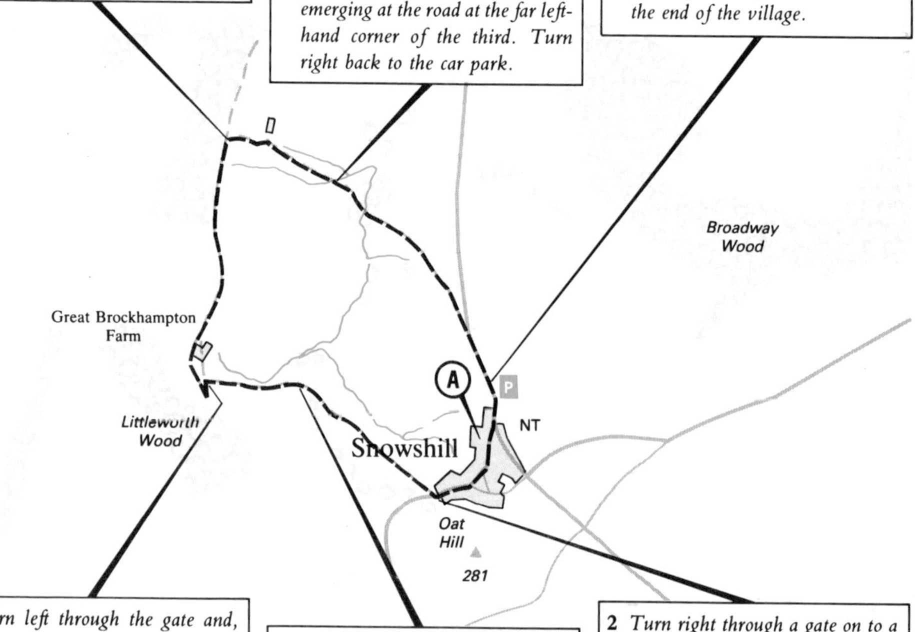

1 *Turn right out of the car park at the northern end of the village and follow the road past the manor to the end of the village.*

2 *Turn right through a gate on to a track. Leave the track at the gate and walk to the left of the fence. Continue alongside the new hedge and plantations to a stile.*

3 *Cross the stile into a large meadow. Walk up the valley heading for the five-bar gate just to the left of the farm.*

4 *Turn left through the gate and, after 100 yards (90 m), double back right on to the tarmac road. Follow it as far as the drive to the second farm on the right.*

5 *Turn right and continue straight on past the farm down the hill to a stile.*

6 *Cross the stile and continue through the woodland. Follow the way-marked stiles up two fields before emerging at the road at the far left-hand corner of the third. Turn right back to the car park.*

A Snowshill Manor is now National Trust property and, in architectural terms, is a good example of a typical fifteenth- to sixteenth-century manor house.

The terraced gardens were laid out in 1919 on the basic design of a cottage garden.

The house once belonged to Charles Wade who acquired not only a West Indian estate but also a very varied collection of items including bicycles, toys, clocks, Japanese armour, farming implements, and musical instruments. He donated these to the Trust and they are on show inside the house.

Walk 18

ULEY AND OWLPEN

3¾ miles (6 km) Moderate; some steep gradients

Uley was a much busier place in the eighteenth century when there were eighteen mills in and around the village. In fact 'Uley Blue' became as well known as the red cloth of the Stroudwater district.

The hillfort above the village is the most spectacular in the Cotswolds and it affords outstanding views over the Severn Vale.

1 *Park in Uley and walk to the post office. Take the tarmac drive to the right then turn right along the footpath near the end. Turn left on the path just after the start of the stone wall. Cross the stile and continue across the field, skirting to the left of the wood, as far as a gate.*

2 *Enter the wood and continue to the left of the metal fence. Cross the stile and head uphill, continuing along the edge to the car park.*

3 *Turn left and follow the path around the next corner to the south-eastern edge of the hill fort.*

4 *Turn right on the path over the hillock and take the left-hand fork at the junction. Cross the stile and follow the tarmac track downhill.*

5 *Turn right at the house and, at the road, turn left to the main road. Turn left as far as South Street on the right.*

6 *Turn right and follow the road past the school. Take the right-hand fork to Sheppard's Mill and continue past the mill to a stile.*

7 *Continue ahead beside the fence to a gate. Go through this and head in the same direction to the next stile. Head uphill to the next stile.*

8 *Turn left to the road. Turn right for about 100 yards (90 m) to a gate and stile on the left just before a house. Cross into the field and continue ahead down to a gate at the corner of the left-hand fence.*

9 *Pass through the gate and head towards the church. Cross the stile and head down to the road. Turn right along the road back to Uley.*

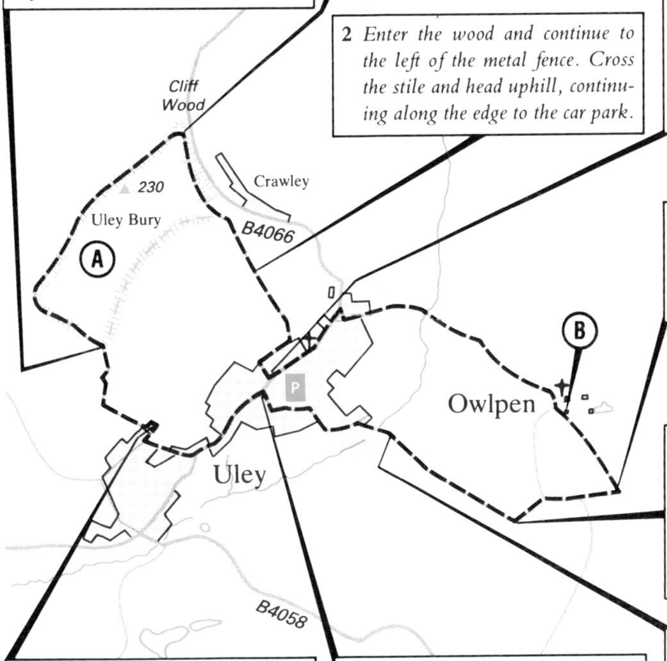

A Uley Bury occupies a superb promontory site with 300-foot (90-m) drops on all sides except the north, and a rampart and ditch providing further protection. It encloses a relatively large area of 30 acres (12 ha), now occupied by a cornfield, and could probably have sheltered up to 2000 Iron Age people.

B Owlpen Manor is regarded as Elizabethan but various parts date from the fifteenth to the eighteenth centuries. It was restored in this century by Norman Jewson.

Walk 19

BREDON HILL

$6\frac{1}{4}$ miles (10 km) Moderate/strenuous; one long climb

Bredon Hill is a detached outlier which pushes the Cotswold frontier well into the Avon Valley. Lying as it does, it is a good indicator of local weather, and generations of forecasters have come up with the rhyme:

When Bredon Hill puts on its hat
Ye men of the Vale beware of that
When Bredon Hill doth clear appear
Ye men of the Vale have naught to fear

The views are superlative, and not only from the top. On the way up, look back to the south to the main plateau and you should easily find the masts on top of Cleeve Hill.

From the summit there are panoramic views to the east, north, and west, looking towards the Malverns, the Vale of Evesham, and over the River Avon, which glints in the sunlight like a silver ribbon as it threads its way through its valley.

Here, in the far north-west corner of the Cotswolds, we are in Worcestershire and the walk begins in Overbury, held by many to be one of the prettiest villages in that county. The presence of many half-timbered buildings is indicative of the proximity of the Midlands. The church is interesting and is one of only sixteen in the country dedicated to St Faith. She was burned on a grid by the Romans in AD 268 for refusing to renounce her faith.

A As might be expected, the natural protection and outlook of the hill proved attractive from very early times.

The hillfort was probably constructed in the Iron Age, and seems to have been the site of a battle. Excavation here revealed the bodies of about fifty men with a superficial covering of earth. They had not been buried and seem to have been left where they fell.

B Given its size and situation, it is unlikely that the Banbury Stone is anything other than a natural outcrop.

At 14 feet ($4\frac{1}{4}$ m) high and with a girth of almost 60 feet ($18\frac{1}{4}$ m), it is a prominent feature that shows evidence of usage. Its historical function is uncertain, however, but it is possible that it may have been a sacrificial stone for the Druids.

As with many other standing stones, there is a legend attached. This one claims that the stone descends down the hill to drink from the Avon each time a clock strikes twelve.

C Here are two more natural outcrops, noted perhaps for their unusual shape and configuration, that possess legendary supernatural powers.

It is said that the King and Queen Stones are a cure for all ailments and that you will invoke their powers and gain good health by passing between the stones. Provided, of course, that you don't slip and break your neck in the process!

Over

Walk 19
Bredon Hill
continued

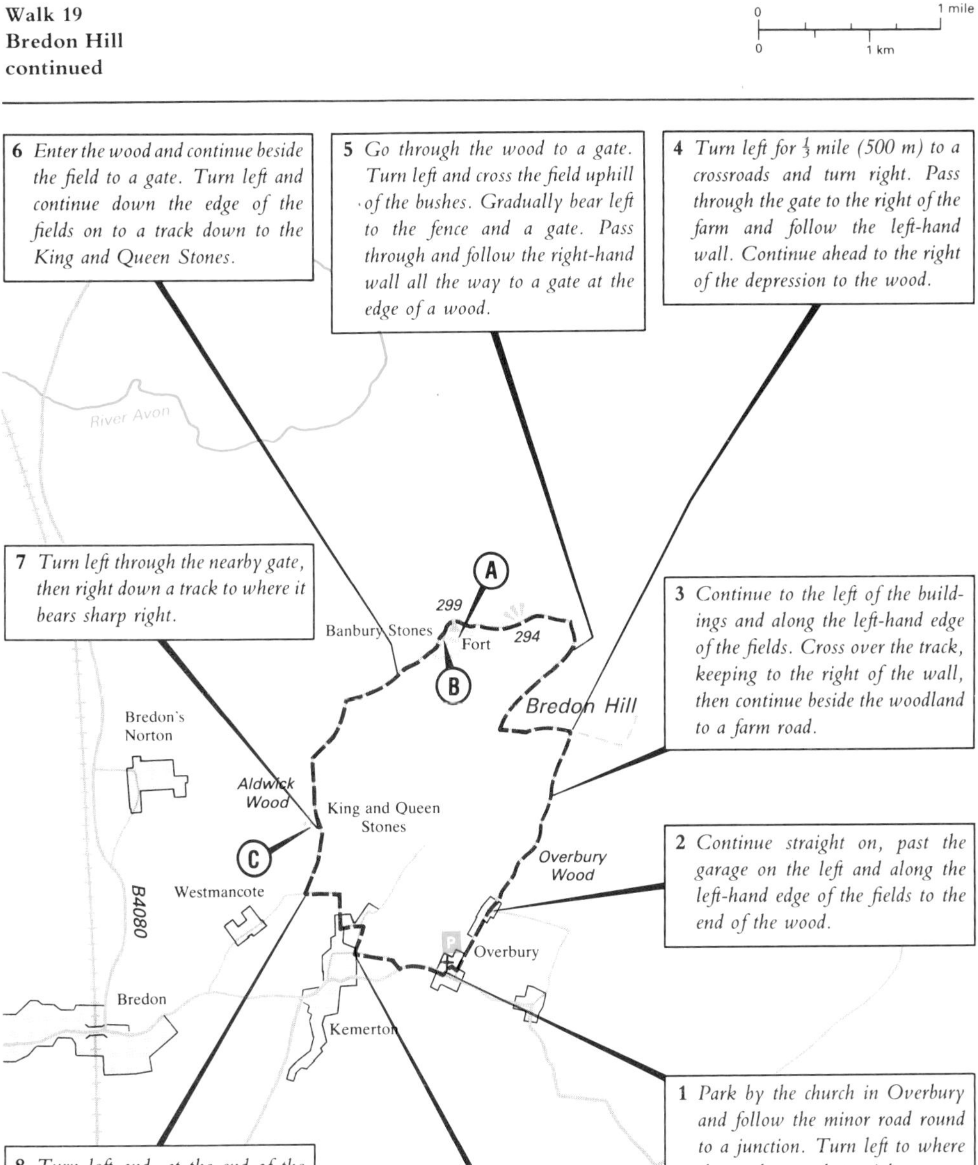

1 *Park by the church in Overbury and follow the minor road round to a junction. Turn left to where the road turns sharp right.*

2 *Continue straight on, past the garage on the left and along the left-hand edge of the fields to the end of the wood.*

3 *Continue to the left of the buildings and along the left-hand edge of the fields. Cross over the track, keeping to the right of the wall, then continue beside the woodland to a farm road.*

4 *Turn left for $\frac{1}{3}$ mile (500 m) to a crossroads and turn right. Pass through the gate to the right of the farm and follow the left-hand wall. Continue ahead to the right of the depression to the wood.*

5 *Go through the wood to a gate. Turn left and cross the field uphill of the bushes. Gradually bear left to the fence and a gate. Pass through and follow the right-hand wall all the way to a gate at the edge of a wood.*

6 *Enter the wood and continue beside the field to a gate. Turn left and continue down the edge of the fields on to a track down to the King and Queen Stones.*

7 *Turn left through the nearby gate, then right down a track to where it bears sharp right.*

8 *Turn left and, at the end of the fields, turn right to the road. Turn left and, at the junction, turn right to a gate on the left by the post box.*

9 *Turn left and, at the next gate, bear half-right to the road. Turn left back into Overbury.*

Walk 20

BLOCKLEY

5¼ miles (8½ km) Moderate; includes one short, busy road section

One of the pleasures of exploration in the Cotswolds is observing the changing colour of the stone. Every town and village has its own characteristic shade of brown, gold, or cream and is usually one of the first things the visitor notices. Here in Blockley the buildings are deep gold with a touch of orange, a hue which imparts a comfortable, warm feeling to the village.

The next thing you may notice is the daily activity in the centre, at a level unusual nowadays for most Cotswold villages. During the week, you can hear children playing in the school, see mothers pushing prams, or watch the local bowls team in action on the green. Blockley seems to be an ordinary community rather than a weekend haunt for outsiders.

It is one of the largest Cotswold villages and one of the least spoilt, containing some fine and historical buildings. It is well worth a look round, and there is an informative guide to the village and its history available in the church.

The route follows the Blockley Brook out of the village into a valley landscaped by John Rushout, Second Lord Northwick. It was given the romantic name of Dovedale in the nineteenth century, possibly after its namesake in the Peak District.

The busy road section is unavoidable but mercifully brief and you soon return to quiet farmland. There are also some lovely stretches of woodland, enjoyable at any time of year but particularly in the spring when they are full of colourful wild flowers. Among others, you will find bluebells, bugle, yellow archangel, vetch, violets, stitchwort, and celandine.

A Blockley has had an interesting history and its fortunes have waxed and waned over the centuries. There was a minster church here by AD 855 responsible for an area of 50 square miles (130 sq km), extending to Morton-in-the-Marsh and Stretton-on-Fosse. The manor house was used by succeeding Bishops of Worcester as a summer residence, and this further boosted the importance of the village.

Like many other Cotswold villages, it suffered with the decline of the wool trade but fared better than most because of the growth of a thriving silk industry. Blockley Brook provided a dependable, adequate water supply which, furthermore, contained enough lime to impart a sheen to the washed silk. The first mill was converted to silk throwing in 1688 and, at the peak of the trade in 1824, there were eight mills employing about 300 women and children plus 3000 homeworkers within a 10-mile (16-km) radius.

The mills specialized in the manufacture of ribbon which was sold mainly to the weavers of Coventry. From 1825 onwards, however, the Blockley trade suffered increasingly from the imports of duty-free French ribbon and, although it staggered on for a few more decades, it ended finally in 1885.

The mills were then put to an amazing variety of uses including the production of cider, rope fibres, soap, cardboard, and pianos. William Morris seriously considered moving his weaving, dyeing, and cotton-printing workshops into one of the old mills but, in the end, decided that it was too far from London.

Most of the old mills have been converted yet again. A good proportion of the houses beside the Blockley Brook at the south end of the village were mills in the seventeenth and eighteenth centuries.

B Five Mile Drive was constructed to improve communications over the wolds between Bourton-on-the-Hill and Broadway. It was built by John Rushout, the same Lord Northwick responsible for the creation of Dovedale.

Over

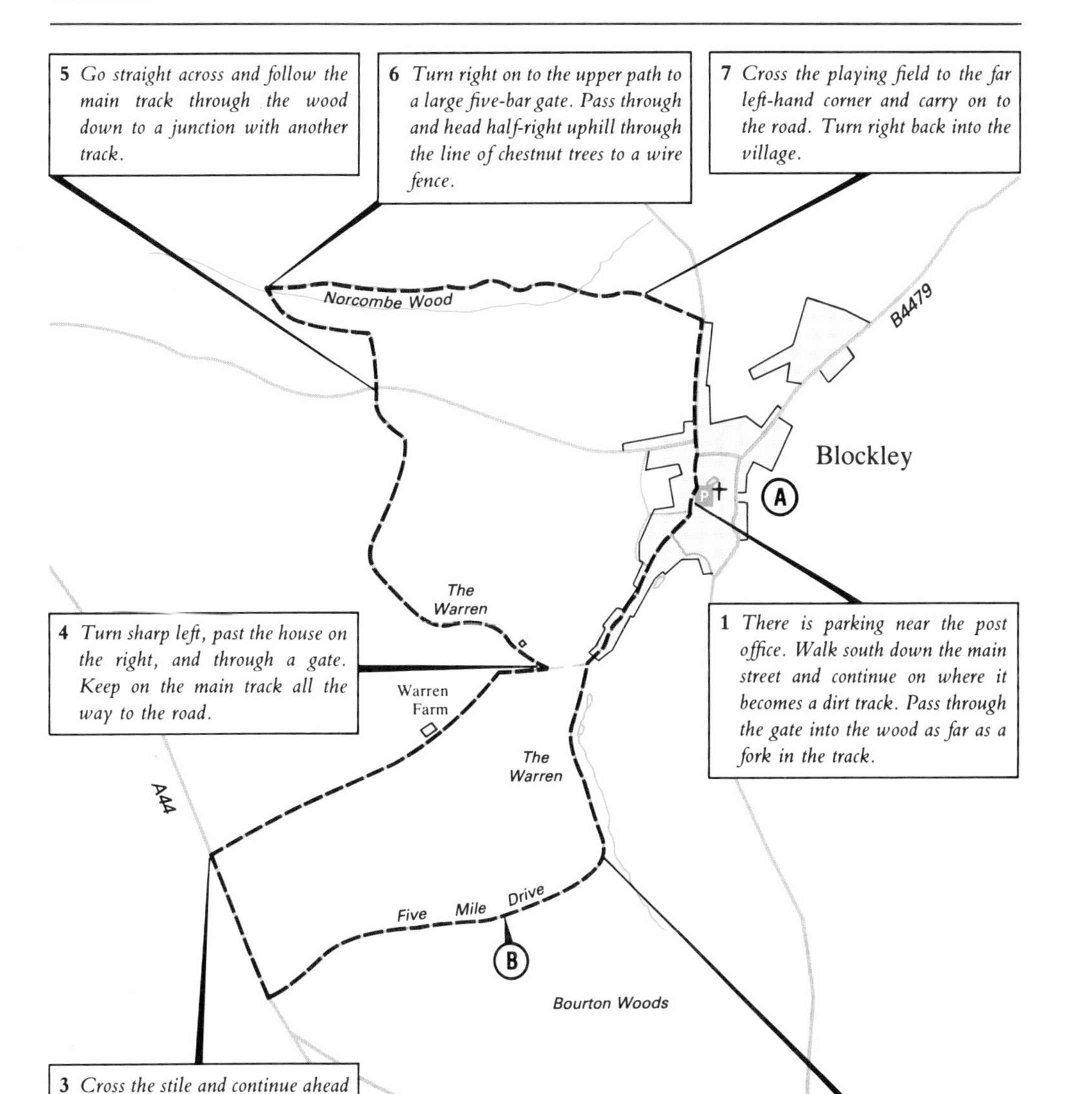
0
1 mile
0
1 km
5 Go straight across and follow the main track through the wood down to a junction with another track.
6 Turn right on to the upper path to a large five-bar gate. Pass through and head half-right uphill through the line of chestnut trees to a wire fence.
7 Cross the playing field to the far left-hand corner and carry on to the road. Turn right back into the village.
Norcombe Wood
B4479
Blockley
A
The Warren
4 Turn sharp left, past the house on the right, and through a gate. Keep on the main track all the way to the road.
Warren Farm
The Warren
1 There is parking near the post office. Walk south down the main street and continue on where it becomes a dirt track. Pass through the gate into the wood as far as a fork in the track.
A44
Five Mile Drive
B
Bourton Woods
3 Cross the stile and continue ahead on the faint path through the fields on to a track. Pass the farm and continue as far as a junction with a gravel drive.
2 Bear right and continue to the road. Turn right for ⅓ mile (500 m) to a waymarked stile on the right.

Walk 21

BOURTON-ON-THE-WATER

$3\frac{3}{4}$ miles (6 km) Moderate; one climb

This is a well-known part of the Windrush valley with crowds flocking every year to admire the attractions of the village frequently described as 'The Venice of the Cotswolds'. We soon see why, with the river flowing wide and shallow through the centre, crossed by low stone bridges most of which are only wide enough for footpaths.

Depending on the mood and inclination of the walker, there are several features in the village which may detain you, but the walk presses on beside the river and explores the valley to the south. The route passes some flooded gravel pits that have become the home for a variety of waterfowl, then ascends the western side of the valley to the small village of Clapton-on-the-Hill, whose church is one of the smallest in the Cotswolds. From here there is a chance to look down into the valley before the gentle descent back into Bourton.

A Bourton's obvious tourist attractions conceal its importance as an archaeological site, for it has had an exceptional historic continuity as a settlement. There is evidence of human habitation since Neolithic times, a period of some 5000 to 6000 years. Just to the east lies Salmonsbury Camp, an Iron Age hillfort that was occupied until Roman times. The Romans crossed the River Windrush here via the Fosse Way, the bridge, of course, having long since decayed. Of the others in the village, the oldest dates back around 200 years. There are several places of interest in Bourton that the walker may wish to visit before or after the walk. Here are a few.

Birdland is a sanctuary containing hundreds of different species of birds, including many exotic varieties such as flamingos and parrots. The penguin collection is particularly good and is considered to be one of the finest in Europe.

The Model Village, now fifty years old, is a replica of Bourton on a scale of 1 to 9. It took four years to construct, and follows the detail of the village faithfully, including a model of the model.

On a similar theme, the model railway covers about 400 square feet (37 sq m) with over forty British and continental trains travelling through a variety of miniature scenery.

Finally, for the mechanically minded, the Motor Museum is possibly an irresistible draw. The museum is broadly set on a 1920s theme and, among the vintage cars and motorcycles, are over 7000 items of memorabilia and a collection of over 600 advertising signs of the period.

Over

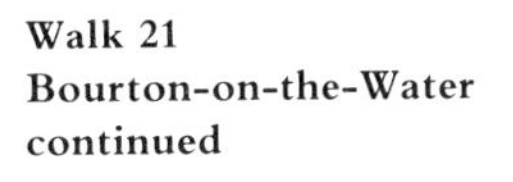

Walk 21 Bourton-on-the-Water continued

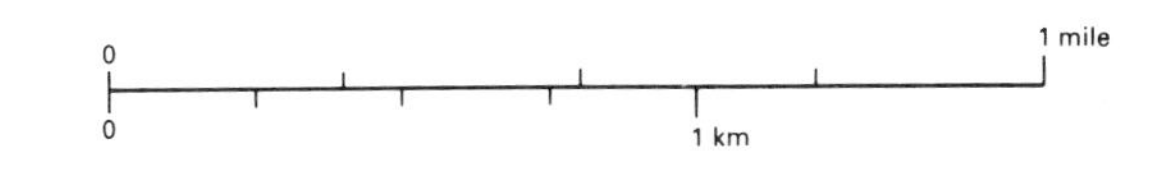

1 *Use the car park beside the main road to the south-east of the village. Turn right out of the car park and continue for about ¼ mile (400 m) as far as Hilcote Drive on the right.*

2 *Turn right, then first left, and, after 50 yards (45 m), turn right down the drive of Applegarth. Cross the stile at the end and continue ahead over a series of stiles to the footbridge across the river.*

3 *Cross over and turn left along the edge of the field to the stiles in the far corner. Cross these, turn right through the gate into the field, and turn left to a stile in front of a barn.*

4 *Turn left over the footbridge, then turn right to the end of the second, smaller lake.*

5 *Turn right, cross the footbridge and stile, then turn right, following the fence all the way to a track. Continue ahead to a junction with another track.*

6 *Continue straight on through a gap in the hedge and walk ahead to the next stile. Continue to the stile at the edge of the plantation.*

7 *Continue to the gate ahead and head slightly to the left across the field to the far gate. Continue up the right-hand edge of the field to a well-defined crossing track. (Turn left if you wish to visit the village.)*

8 *Turn right and follow the track all the way to a small field. Cross this to the stile ahead.*

9 *Cross the stile and continue straight ahead over several fields and way-marked stiles, eventually following the left-hand field boundaries to a footbridge on the left.*

10 *Cross over and turn half-right. Cross the next footbridge and continue ahead over the way-marked stiles to the road, then turn right back into the village.*

Bourton-on-the-Water
A
P
Nethercote
B4068
River Dikler
Clapton Gorse
Lower Marsh Farm
Clapton-on-the-Hill

Walk 22

CHIPPING CAMPDEN AND DOVER'S HILL

$4\frac{1}{4}$ miles ($6\frac{3}{4}$ km) Moderate; two climbs (one steep), some mud

The beautiful curving High Street and imposing church of Chipping Campden are two major features of the Cotswolds. Many of the town's buildings date from the time of James I and earlier, while the church is arguably the finest in the Cotswolds. This alone should indicate that the walk could take appreciably longer than its length implies. But there are other features along the route, including a lovely section of woodland and the viewpoint from Dover's Hill – an incentive for the steep pull from the valley.

A 'Chipping' is found elsewhere in the Cotswolds and derives from the Saxon *ceping* for a market. This was to prove very appropriate, for the town later established itself as a market centre for wool, rather than for production of the woven cloth.

The fourteenth-century Woolstaplers Hall was the meeting place of the staple merchants where they purchased the raw fleece. The most famous of the merchants was William Grevel, mentioned by Chaucer in *Canterbury Tales*. His fourteenth-century house remains almost unaltered in the High Street.

Like Painswick, Chipping Campden suffered from the emergence of the Stroud area, and the town went into a steady decline. A disaster at the time, perhaps, but it has preserved the appearance of the town for us today.

Another important local figure was Sir Baptist Hicks, a merchant banker, who built the Market Hall in 1627 for the butter and cheese market. He also built the attractive row of almshouses near the church in 1612. The church was built following a bequest by William Grevel, and is almost entirely fifteenth century, lending it a unity of style. There are several notable features inside, particularly the brass of William Grevel and his wife, among the largest and oldest of Gloucestershire brasses.

B This very historic spot was a 'moot' point where the local people discussed business and dispensed justice. Part of its name derives from the Saxon word for track – *geat* – but it was probably in use before those times.

Magna Carta was read from the stone as were the proclamations of monarchs, the last one being that of George III.

C Whitsun Games were probably held on the hill as far back as Saxon times but it was later the site of the famous Cotswold 'Olympick' Games, begun by Robert Dover in 1612.

They were certainly not for the weak in body or spirit, involving such activities as wrestling, handwalking, shinkicking, and a particularly rough pursuit called singlestick fighting. In this event, competitors tucked one hand into the belt and held a long stick in the other, the aim being to 'break the others head'. Some contests lasted for hours. There was also hare coursing, foot racing, and games of cards and chess housed in tents. The occasion became very popular and, in the 1830s, as many as 30 000 people attended.

Unfortunately, the Games became unruly, attracting the criminal elements of society. A series of riots in the middle of the nineteenth century excited by nearby railway workers led to demands for the event to be cancelled, and the Games were finally stopped in 1853.

The land was acquired by the National Trust in 1928 but includes only part of the area occupied by the Games. They were revived in 1951, although not including all of the original events, and take place at Whitsuntide.

Over

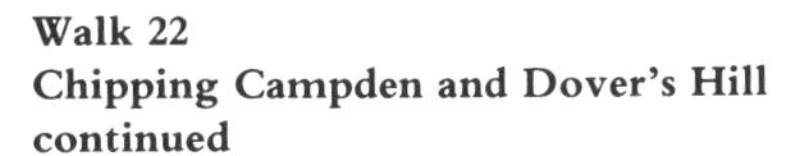

Walk 22
Chipping Campden and Dover's Hill continued

1 *Park in Chipping Campden. From the main street turn down Back Ends and Hoo Lane. At the sharp right-hand bend, take the first turning on the left and continue over the road to the corner of the field. Take the path half-right uphill to the road.*

2 *Turn right and, after ¼ mile (400 m), take the path half-left across the field to Broadway Tower. At the road, turn left, past the Kiftsgate Stone on the right, to a junction.*

3 *Bear right and continue for ¼ mile (400 m) to a bridleway on the right just after a right-hand bend.*

4 *Turn right and go downhill, keeping close to the right-hand field boundaries when the track emerges from the wood. Re-enter the woodland and look out for a stile when a field comes into view on the right.*

5 *Cross the stile and head half-left across the field. Cross the stile near the corner and turn right uphill, crossing a track, to the stile in the top corner of the field.*

6 *Continue in the same direction over the next stile to a hedge. Turn left to the road.*

7 *Turn right, and, after 300 yards (275 m), take the path on the left to Dover's Hill. Go straight on over the summit, crossing the stile ahead and continuing to the road.*

8 *Turn left and take the second path on the right (the Cotswold Way) back into Chipping Campden.*

The Lynches Wood
NT
Dover's Hill
230
Chipping Campden
Cotswold Way
Weston Park
B4035
Kiftsgate Stone
Campden Wood

Walk 23

HARESFIELD BEACON

4 miles ($6\frac{1}{2}$ km) Moderate

There is a lot packed into this relatively short walk with plenty of beautiful scenery to capture your attention. Allow extra time to admire the views and to linger in the lovely woodland, especially in the spring and summer when there occurs the riotous mixture of blues, yellows, and pinks of bluebells, yellow archangel, and campion. The accompanying sweet woodruff and wood spurge seem very sober in comparison.

Standish Wood and Haresfield Beacon stand on westerly facing promontories overlooking the Severn valley. The defensive virtues of the sites appealed to people from very early times, and Randwick Long Barrow at the southern end of the wood is dated at 3000 to 2500 BC. There are also three Bronze Age tumuli built around 1000 BC and, of course, there is the hillfort on Haresfield Hill constructed during the Iron Age.

Standish Wood is very old, first recorded in 1297 as belonging to Gloucester Abbey. In fact, the whole area used to be much more heavily wooded but it was extensively cleared during World War 1. There was a further threat in 1930 from developers but local people managed to raise the funds to buy 327 acres (132 ha), which they then gave to the National Trust. The Trust has since planted a mixture of coniferous and deciduous trees and extended its ownership to over 420 acres (170 ha).

A This stone is known locally as Cromwell's Stone, erected to commemorate the success of the Parliamentarians in raising the siege of Gloucester in 1643. In July of that year Prince Rupert captured Bristol, leaving Gloucester as an isolated Parliamentarian stronghold in the west of England. King Charles also wanted to open up the River Severn as a supply artery and he surrounded the city on 5 August. It held out for a month, however, until reinforcements arrived under the Earl of Essex – around 15 000 men in all. The King decided it prudent to withdraw and gave the Roundheads one of their few successes in the early part of the Civil War.

Why the stone was placed here is not known for certain but, if the trees behind were cleared, there would be an excellent view of Gloucester.

B As at Uley Bury, the hillfort has utilized the natural defences of the promontory. The outlook is excellent with steep slopes on three sides and the fourth closed off by a rampart and ditch across the neck of land to the east. It covers about 16 acres (6½ ha) in all and so well sited that the Romans made use of it in their military campaigns. Numerous Roman artefacts have been uncovered, including a collection of 3000 coins.

C From the triangulation point at the end of Ring Hill, there is a superb view of the escarpment, and probably the best outlook over the Berkeley Vale.

Several outliers are visible, including Churchdown, Robin Wood's Hill, and Stinchcombe Hill. In the distance is the Forest of Dean, forming a backdrop to the Severn below, and in good conditions, it is possible to see the Severn Bridge.

Over

Walk 23
Haresfield Beacon
continued

0 1 mile
0 1 km

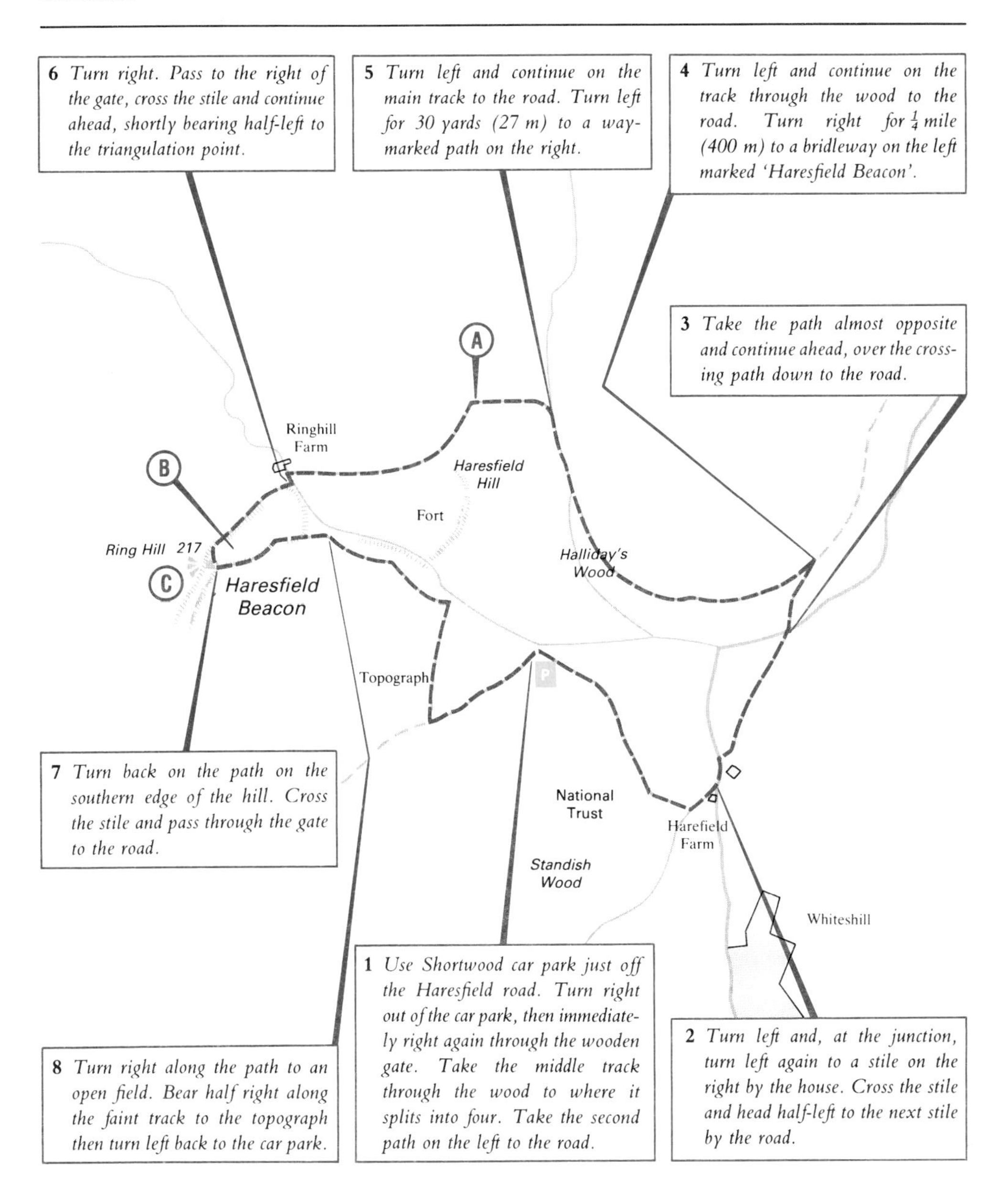

Walk 24

PAINSWICK AND PAINSWICK BEACON

5 miles (8 km) Moderate

Painswick is one of the loveliest of the Cotswold towns. It is largely constructed from the creamy local stone and possesses considerable unity and 'wholeness', thus earning its title as 'Queen of the Cotswolds'.

The route begins in the town, which can easily absorb several hours of exploration. It then crosses the golf course – definitely the most hazardous part of the route – to reach the Beacon and the viewpoint.

It returns to Painswick via Paradise, not quite as promising as it sounds but with an interesting background. In the eighteenth century, there was a small weaving centre here, but the unusual name derives from the local pub sign which depicted Adam and Eve in Paradise. The route passes the old inn, which was called The Adam and Eve, and through the small village that was called Paradise.

A Painswick acquired its modern name relatively late, since the Anglo Saxon 'wicke' was named in the twelfth century after Pain Fitzjohn, the lord of the manor.

The town's prosperity came from wool, and cloth was being manufactured by the mid-fifteenth century. There was a thriving weaving industry by the seventeenth century and, at its peak, there were a dozen or so mills in the valley with many looms in the town. The local clear, soft water and the presence of woad led to a specialization in dyeing skills, and Painswick became known throughout Europe for its coloured cloth. Exports fell in the eighteenth century, however, and the local clothiers, unable to raise the capital for the new machines introduced later in the century, lost out to the bigger concerns in the Stroud valley.

The town's population fell as families moved away to find work elsewhere and, by the early nineteenth century, the wool trade was almost dead. As in many other wool towns, the financial restraints and disasters after the collapse of the industry preserved the physical structure of the community from unsympathetic development.

There are several notable buildings, especially the group of fourteenth-century houses in Bisley Street – The Chur, Little Fleece, and Wickstone. The post office is a fifteenth-century timber-framed house. The town is full of historic buildings, however, and the interested walker is recommended to buy the town guide.

The churchyard is famous for its yews and tombs. The oldest of the yews were planted in 1792, and one local legend has it that there are ninety-nine and that a hundredth always dies. Another says they can't be counted to the same number twice.

On 19 September each year, there occurs the Clipping Ceremony when the church is circled by children singing a traditional hymn. The event happens to coincide with trimming the yews but the name derives from the Saxon *ycleping* meaning to encircle or embrace. The ceremony first occurred in 1897 although it probably has ancient, pagan origins.

The table-top tombs are the finest in the Cotswolds and mainly the work of the Bryans family. Guides are available in the church. The church also houses a well-known peal of bells, increased to twelve in 1821 in response, it is said, to Stroud's increased complement of ten. There has traditionally been much rivalry between 'Proud Painswick' and 'Strutting Stroud'.

B Quarrying has extensively damaged the ramparts of the fort, described in a text of 1907 as a 'wonder to behold'. It has two entrances and an overall triangular shape. The summit is at 930 feet (283 m) and overlooks the Severn valley.

Over

Walk 24
Painswick and Painswick Beacon continued

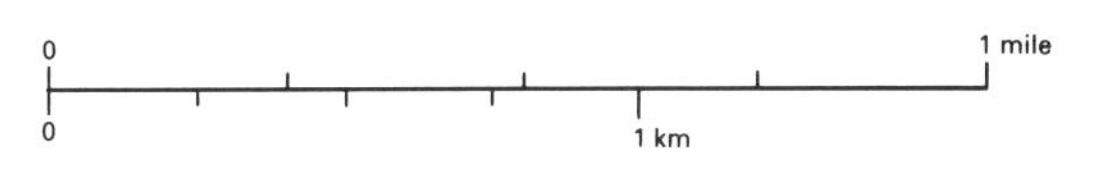

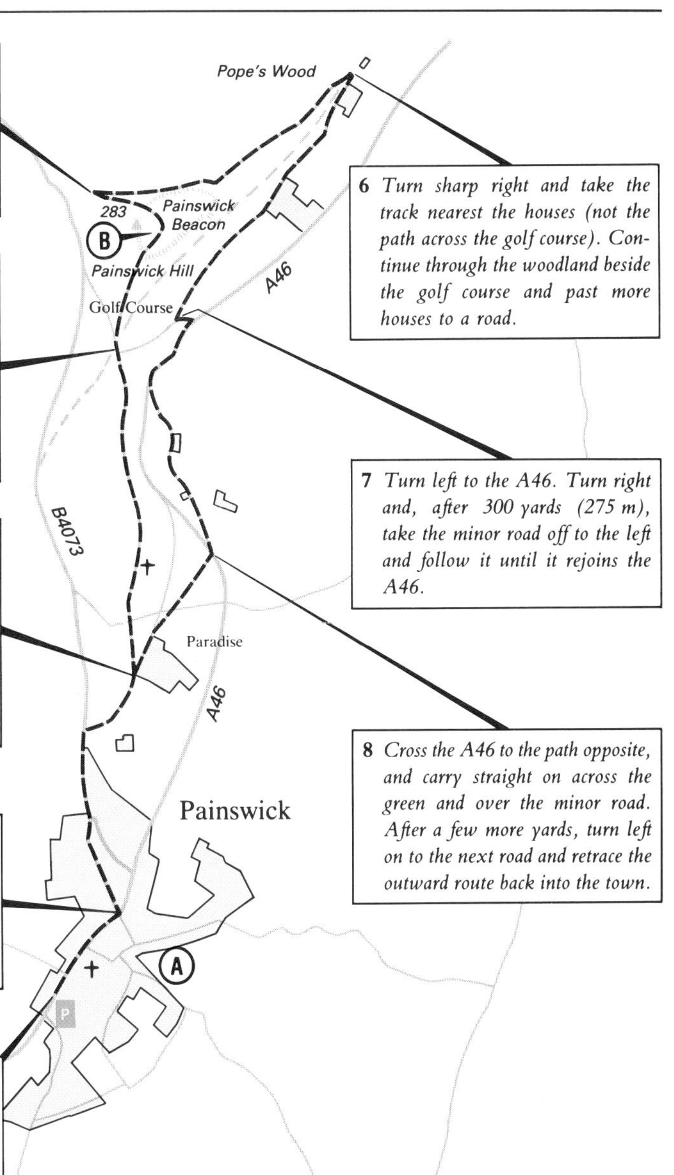

1 *Use the car park off the A46 at the southern end of Painswick. Follow the A46 back into the town to the traffic lights at the crossroads.*

2 *Turn left on to the Gloucester road. Follow this for* $\frac{1}{3}$ *mile (500 m) to Golf Club Road on the right. Turn right and continue for 300 yards (275 m) to a green and footpath sign on the left.*

3 *Turn half-left (do not follow the wall) and cross the green. Go straight on over the road, then keep to the left of the cemetery wall. At the corner, cross the green to the wood ahead and follow the path past the quarry to the road.*

4 *Turn left for 75 yards (68 m) and then right on to a track. After 100 yards (90 m), take the minor left fork uphill. Skirt around to the right of the triangulation pillar, then follow the path westwards and downhill to a junction with a track just before the road.*

5 *Turn sharp right and follow the track along the hillside, going straight on at a junction by the garage, and eventually following the edge of the golf course to some houses.*

6 *Turn sharp right and take the track nearest the houses (not the path across the golf course). Continue through the woodland beside the golf course and past more houses to a road.*

7 *Turn left to the A46. Turn right and, after 300 yards (275 m), take the minor road off to the left and follow it until it rejoins the A46.*

8 *Cross the A46 to the path opposite, and carry straight on across the green and over the minor road. After a few more yards, turn left on to the next road and retrace the outward route back into the town.*

Walk 25

OZLEWORTH

2 miles ($3\frac{1}{4}$ km) Easy

0 — 1 mile
0 — 1 km

This must be one of the quietest parts of the Cotswolds, often with nothing but the farm animals and the wildlife to break the silence. Once enveloped inside the woodland, it is hard to imagine that you are barely a mile (1½ km) from the car.

Ozleworth is hardly a village at all, just a few buildings surrounding the eighteenth-century manor house. Indeed, you have to wonder at the presence of the church in such an isolated spot. The present belies the past, however, for the area was once relatively heavily populated.

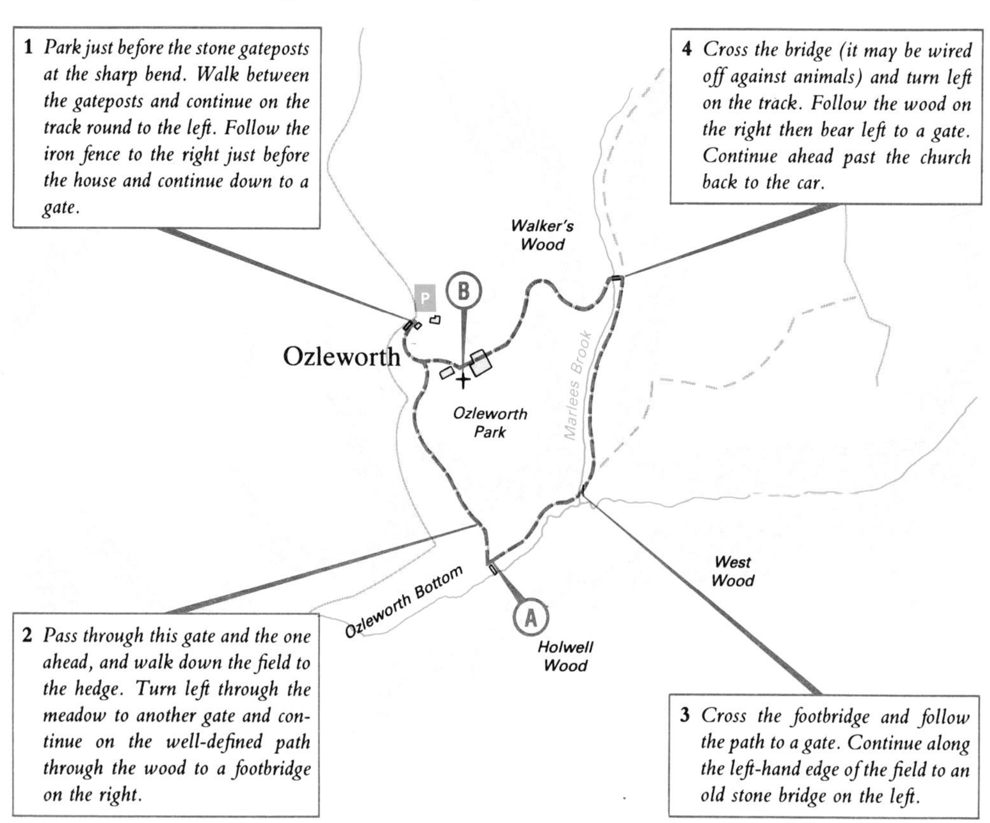

A Incredibly, this row of cottages is the remains of a community once 1600 strong, attracted by the wool industry. The nearby Little Avon River had sufficient strength to power many mills in this area.

B This largely Norman church is remarkable for several features. It stands in a circular church yard, almost 150 feet (45 m) in diameter, that clearly exceeded the parish requirements. The church is thought to have been placed in a pre-Christian ritual site.

The most striking feature is probably the rare six-sided tower, but there is also some superb stone carving on the south doorway and on the west tower arch.

Walk 26

MINCHINHAMPTON

5 miles (8 km) Easy

0 — 1 mile
0 — 1 km

This is an almost level route, but its hilltop location affords fine views over the neighbouring Frome and Nailsworth valleys.

This is one of the largest areas of common land south of Cleeve Hill and it is now owned by the National Trust. It was used for grazing sheep as far back as Norman times, and the walker may still have to wend his or her way through the livestock.

1 *Park the car in Minchinhampton and make your way to the church. Walk down Bell Lane past the church, then turn right to the edge of the common.*

2 *Turn left and follow the left-hand wall to the road. Go straight across and, at the corner of the wall, carry straight on to the right of the house ahead to the road.*

3 *Cross over, then shortly bear right across the golf course to the road. Turn left and take the track on the right to the Old Lodge Inn.*

4 *Turn right across the common, crossing the road about 100 yards (90 m) to the right of the bend, and head towards the right-hand side of the houses at the edge of the common.*

5 *Walk ahead to the war memorial for the view, then recross the road and follow the wall beside the houses on the left. At the corner, continue straight on across the common to the road and turn right. When convenient bear left downhill across the common to the road.*

6 *Turn left, then turn right into the lane just past the telephone box as far as a junction.*

7 *Go straight on, then straight on again after another 50 yards (45 m). Bear left at the next junction and continue straight on to the footpath along the edge of the common as far as a crossing path.*

8 *Turn right across the field to the left of the boundary. Cross the drive and continue to the road. Turn right and then go straight on at the crossroads back into Minchinhampton.*

A Minchinhampton grew up as a cloth town but was also an important stone producer. By the eighteenth century, it was a leading cloth manufacturer but, by the nineteenth century, workers descended the hill to work in the new factories of the Stroud valley. Note the seventeenth-century Market Hall in the town centre.

B These are the remains of an Iron Age hillfort that defended some 600 acres (243 ha). The Romans may have destroyed the fort after meeting local resistance here.

Walk 27

SYDE AND BRIMPSFIELD

$5\frac{3}{4}$ miles ($9\frac{1}{4}$ km) Moderate

If you wish to escape the crowds and bustle of everyday life, or indeed just prefer walking by yourself, you could do worse than to choose this route. It follows the valley of the infant Frome almost to its source, and it seems incredible that downstream this peaceful stretch of water – here little more than a brook – once helped to power the mighty cloth industry of Stroud.

The route passes through small villages one of which, Brimpsfield, is said to have the smallest post office in England. As in other places in the Cotswolds – Ozleworth Bottom, for instance – present appearances do not necessarily reflect the historical importance of a particular place. Two-hundred-and-fifty years ago Caudle Green was the site of a notable spinning house that employed many of the women and children of the area.

The walk begins in Syde, a rare village name for the south and Midlands of England that derives from the Saxon *side* describing the long hill slope falling away from the village down to the river.

Before you leave the village, it is worth visiting the church, which contains Anglo-Saxon work over the south doorway. This was closed in the fourteenth century, and the building now has to be entered from the north side.

The attractive saddleback tower is not uncommon in this district and was added in the thirteenth or fourteenth century.

Nearby is the fourteenth-century tithe barn used for storing the crops, fleeces, timber, and hides levied for the Abbeys of Gloucester and Cirencester. Unfortunately, it was damaged by fire but some of the original building remains.

A Only the irregular surface of the field below the church now indicates the site of the 700-year-old castle built by John Gifford. Gifford rebelled unsuccessfully against King Edward II in 1322, and the castle was slighted. The process was completed by the locals who plundered the ruins for building stone, and only the foundation stones and moats have survived.

Over

Walk 27
Syde and Brimpsfield
continued

1 *Park in Syde (spaces near the church) and turn down the road marked 'Syde — No through road'. Turn right before the wooden gates, then continue beside the stone wall. Where this ends, bear half-right downhill to the fence and turn right. Go over the stile, cross the stream, and continue by the fence to a small gate.*

2 *Turn right through the gate, cross the footbridge, then turn left on the path through the wood as far as a stile in the fence. Cross the stile and continue to the gate just ahead on the left.*

3 *Turn left through the gate and continue on the track, through the farm, to the road. Turn right as far as Stoneway House on the right.*

4 *Turn left along the No through road opposite, then take the right-hand path beside the wall (past the post office). Continue ahead across the field and along the right-hand edge of the next fields to the road.*

5 *Continue along the right-hand edge of the fields and pass through the wood. Continue along the edge of the field to the next wood, over the stile to a track. Turn left and cross the stile at the roadside.*

6 *Turn left along the road for 20 yards (18 m), then right along a path to a well-defined track.*

7 *Turn right, pass to the left of the pond, and take the left-hand fork where the track splits. At the next fork, take the right-hand path. At the marshy area, follow the path away from the stream to a gate.*

8 *Turn right, take the left-hand path where the track splits, and continue to next fork.*

9 *Take the left-hand path uphill and continue to the open field at the edge of the wood.*

10 *Bear slightly left and head for the buildings in the far corner. Continue past these to the road.*

11 *Turn right and, just after the last house, turn left over a stile down the field to the road. Continue ahead for 75 yards (68 m) to a drive on the right.*

12 *Turn right, continue past the farm and over two stiles by the Wellingtonia trees. Head half-right uphill to the stone wall and retrace your steps to the car.*

Ermin Way
ROMAN ROAD
A417
A
Castle (site of)
Hazel Hanger Wood
Brimpsfield
Climperwell Farm
Groveridge Hill
Poston Wood
Climperwell Wood
Syde
Whiteway
Caudle Green
New Seal Wood
River Frome

Walk 28

CASTLE COMBE

$4\frac{3}{4}$ miles ($7\frac{1}{2}$ km) Moderate; some mud

Castle Combe is one of the most famous and picturesque villages in the Cotswolds. It has been used as a location for several films, but the surrounding countryside is just as attractive. The walk contains some lovely woodland and meadow and an interesting side valley.

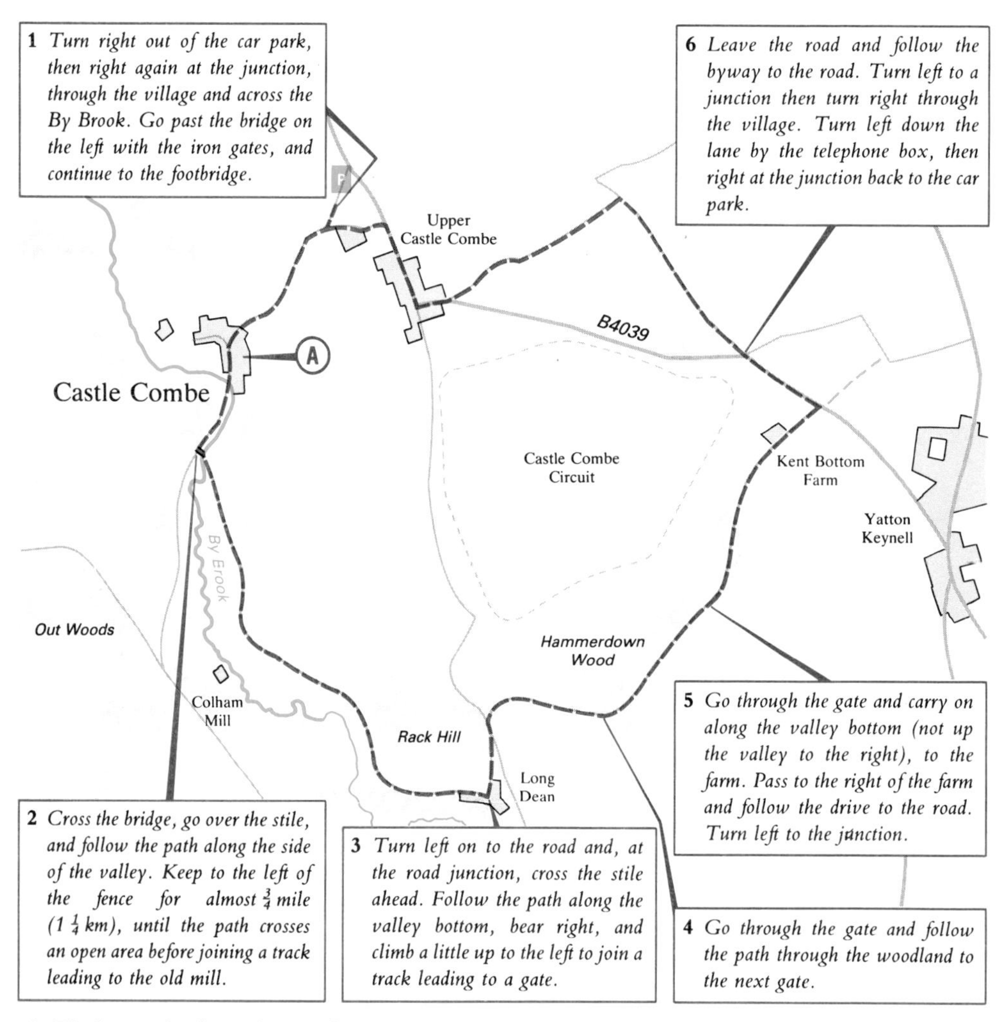

1 *Turn right out of the car park, then right again at the junction, through the village and across the By Brook. Go past the bridge on the left with the iron gates, and continue to the footbridge.*

2 *Cross the bridge, go over the stile, and follow the path along the side of the valley. Keep to the left of the fence for almost $\frac{3}{4}$ mile ($1\frac{1}{4}$ km), until the path crosses an open area before joining a track leading to the old mill.*

3 *Turn left on to the road and, at the road junction, cross the stile ahead. Follow the path along the valley bottom, bear right, and climb a little up to the left to join a track leading to a gate.*

4 *Go through the gate and follow the path through the woodland to the next gate.*

5 *Go through the gate and carry on along the valley bottom (not up the valley to the right), to the farm. Pass to the right of the farm and follow the drive to the road. Turn left to the junction.*

6 *Leave the road and follow the byway to the road. Turn left to a junction then turn right through the village. Turn left down the lane by the telephone box, then right at the junction back to the car park.*

A Wool was the basis for the village's wealth, the By Brook powering the cloth mills.

The village was noted for its sheep fair, attracting flocks from as far as Northamptonshire.

The ruined Norman castle to the north gave the village the first part of its name.

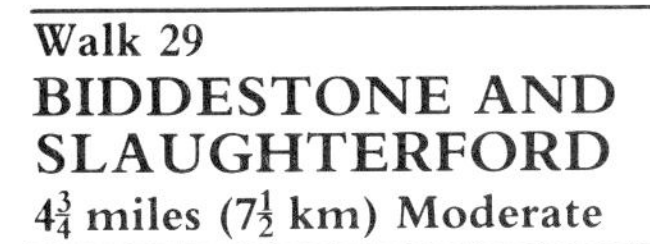

Walk 29

BIDDESTONE AND SLAUGHTERFORD

$4\frac{3}{4}$ miles ($7\frac{1}{2}$ km) Moderate

There are no major architectural masterpieces or panoramic views on this route – it is simply a very pleasant walk through small villages and very attractive meadows. Do not be put off by the road section, for the lanes are very quiet.

The pond and waterfowl form the visual centrepiece of Biddestone, a spot that bids you to linger. Slaughterford was probably named similarly to the other more famous Slaughters, as 'the ford by the sloe trees'.

1 *Leave the car in Biddestone. At the road junction by the village pond, take the road to Hartham. Go past the church and, where the road forks, bear right. Follow the road for over a mile ($1\frac{1}{2}$ km) to the junction at the bottom of the steep hill.*

2 *Turn right and follow the road past the paper mills to the road junction by the bridge. Turn right for 150 yards (135 m) to the sharp right-hand bend.*

3 *Take the footpath ahead (note the old water wheel on the right) and cross the footbridges. Follow the path through the meadow to the gated weir.*

4 *Cross the weir and go half-left across the meadow to a gap in the corner. Follow the path ahead, staying close to the river, crossing a fence and over another field to a weir in the corner.*

5 *Cross the footbridge and head for the corner of the field. Cross the stile to the road and turn right as far as the White Hart Inn. Turn right and, after 200 yards (180 m), take the left fork and carry on up to a junction.*

6 *Bear left, then right after 300 yards (275 m) at the next junction. After $\frac{3}{4}$ mile ($1\frac{1}{4}$ km), turn right into Biddestone.*

Ford
Toplands Farm
A420
Common Hill
122
By Brook
Slaughterford
Backpath Wood
Paper Mills
Coombs Woods
Biddestone
A

A The earliest parts of Biddestone church were completed by the middle of the twelfth century. Its most notable feature, however, is the Early English bell turret, the lower section built in the thirteenth century and the remainder in the fifteenth.

Its two small bells are medieval, one of which until recently had spent 100 years in a farmyard.

Walk 30

FROCESTER HILL AND HETTY PEGLER'S TUMP

4 miles (6½ km) Moderate; one steep climb, some mud

There are wonderful views over the Severn Vale from the edge of the escarpment at Frocester Hill, and the panorama dial puts names to distant features. You can begin to appreciate the view the pilots of the gliders and hangliders must have from their craft after taking off from the hilltop.

Vertigo sufferers will probably prefer to concentrate on things nearer to hand, and there is certainly plenty of interest on this walk.

To reach the viewpoint from the car, the route crosses some delightful meadowland which, in spring and summer, is covered with sainfoin and orchids, among others. It is part of the nature reserve owned by the National Trust and formed to protect the limestone grassland and its typical flora and fauna.

There are also two important archaeological sites and some lovely woodland to enjoy along the way.

A Nympsfield Long Barrow is an example of the earlier, true-entranced Cotswold-Severn style, constructed around 2500 BC. Unfortunately, it had already been partly destroyed before the first proper excavation in 1862, but at least the lack of a roof offers the chance of examining the general layout.

A short passage from the eastern end leads to three chambers where the remains of sixteen skeletons and pottery were found in the 1862 excavation.

The mound was surrounded by a low dry stone wall, most of which has now been reconstructed. The upright slabs, however, are original.

B Hetty Pegler's Tump, in common with Belas Knap, is of particular interest because it is still roofed. This is an example of the later, false-entranced Neolithic tomb and is virtually intact, although some parts have been reconstructed. It is 140 feet (42½ m) long and 90 feet (27½ m) wide, and inside there are two pairs of side chambers off a central passage 22 feet (6½ m) long.

The door is kept locked to protect the monument but the key can be obtained at Crawley Barns, passed earlier on along the route.

For reasons still uncertain, it was named after Hester Pegler, the wife of the man who owned the field in the seventeenth century. She probably took an interest in the barrow and may even have organized an opening. The tomb is known to have been opened several times, and nineteenth-century excavations revealed Roman pottery and a fifteenth-century coin.

Over

Walk 30
Frocester Hill and Hetty Pegler's Tump continued

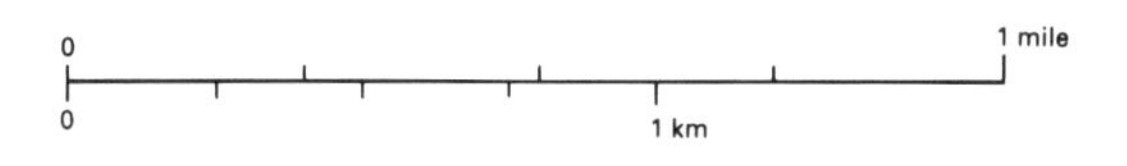

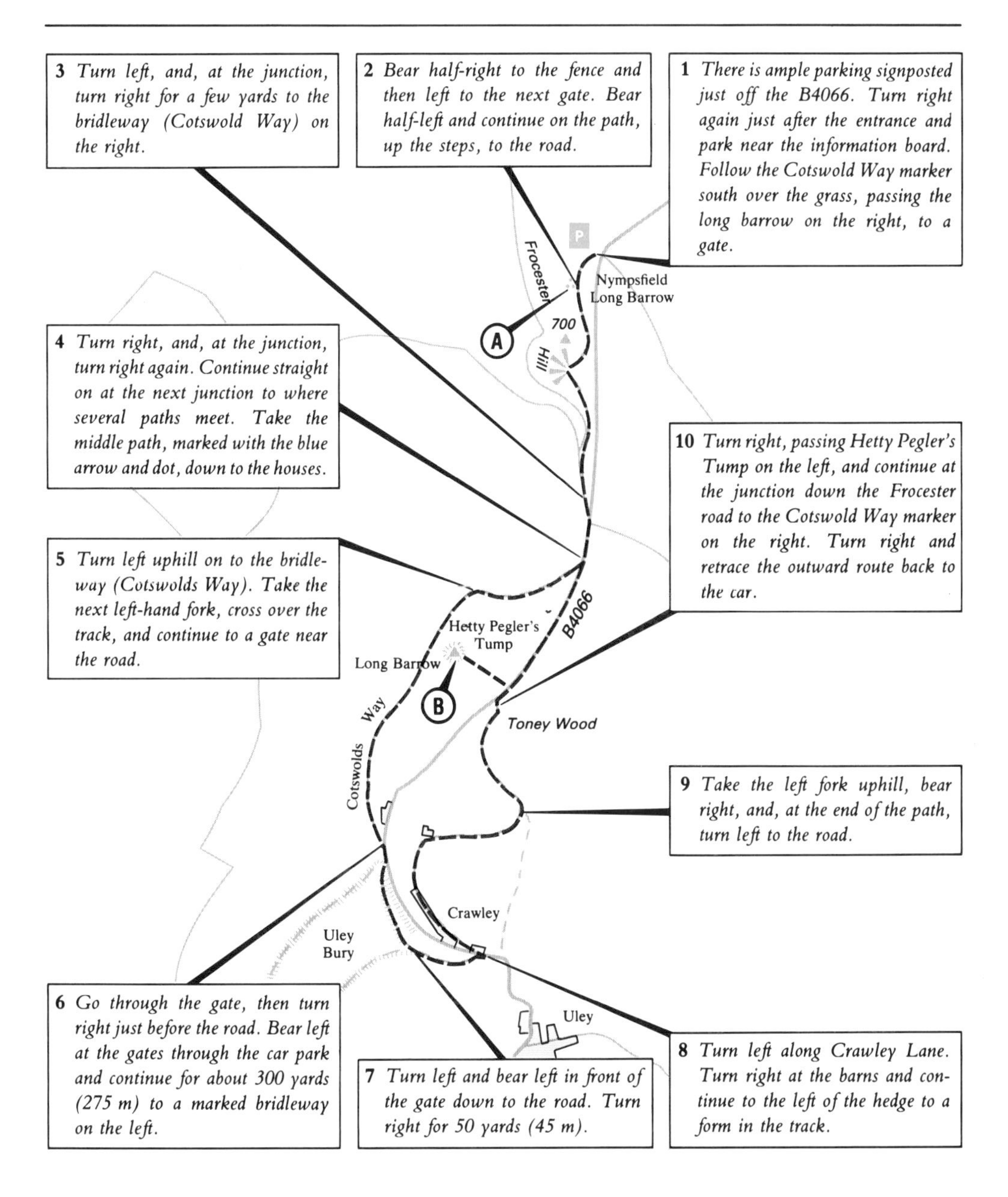

Walk 31

WOTTON-UNDER-EDGE AND THE TYNDALE MONUMENT

4½ miles (7¼ km) Moderate; muddy in places

This route follows the Cotswold Way through the lovely woodland to the north of Wotton-under-Edge, and emerges, rather suddenly, on to the open grassland of Nibley Knoll. The view over the Severn Vale is wonderful from here and makes a suitable pivot point for the return journey.

The walk begins in Wotton which, in both the literal and physical sense, lies under the escarpment edge. Its full title of 'under-Edge' was added to its Saxon prefix much later, in the fourteenth century. It came to prominence with the growth of the wool trade, becoming one of the most important wool towns in the Cotswolds. An influx of Flemish weavers gave the industry a boost and, by the early seventeenth century, the trade was well established, with half the working population involved in some way with the production of cloth.

Serious riots in 1825 were indicative of the decline of the trade in the nineteenth century, but the town managed to foster other local industries and today houses a thriving community. It also managed to preserve much of its finest architectural heritage, and the ancient street, called The Chipping, with its sixteenth-century timbered houses and eighteenth-century town hall, received an architectural award.

In Church Street, there is an attractive row of seventeenth-century almshouses while, elsewhere, the elegant eighteenth-century houses of the wealthy merchants flank the streets. There are plenty of other noteworthy buildings in the town for those with an interest in architecture.

The tower of the largely fifteenth-century church is held by some to be one of the finest in the county. Inside are the famous life-size brasses of Thomas Berkeley and his wife Margaret. They are thought to date from the time of Margaret's death in 1392 and may well have been the work of the same craftsman of the Russel brass at Dyrham.

The organ was constructed in about 1720 and originally belonged to St Martin in the Fields, London, where it was frequently played by Handel. The church acquired it in 1800 when it was put up for sale.

Wotton has had some famous residents. Edward Jenner, the discoverer of vaccination, was a native of the town, and it was while teaching here from 1837–39 that Isaac Pitman developed his famous system of shorthand.

A The trees mostly obscure the form and structure of the Iron Age hillfort but it is still an atmospheric site. The ditches and ramparts enclosed a roughly triangular area of 6 acres (2½ ha), protected on two sides by the scarp slope and a double ditch and rampart on the third side at the neck.

B The monument was erected in 1866 in memory of William Tyndale, who was born near here some time between 1490 and 1495. He was greatly concerned that the ordinary people should be able to follow the Bible in English and began translating the New Testament in the early 1520s.

His work and unorthodox views attracted much criticism, and he felt it prudent to continue his labours abroad in Hamburg. The work was completed in 1526 and, in 1530, he commenced work on the Old Testament. Despite the changing religious climate in England, however, he was imprisoned, charged with heresy, and executed in Flanders in 1536.

It is a sad irony that, just two years after Tyndale's death, Henry VIII ordered that every church in England should have an English Bible.

C These are the remains of strip lynchets – an ancient method of farming sloping land. Earth would be extracted from one edge of the terrace and deposited at the other to smooth out the contours and create areas of flatter land that could be more easily cultivated. The lynchets are of uncertain age.

Over

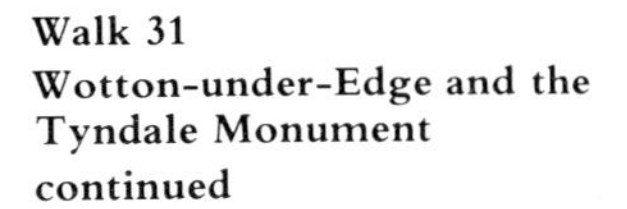

Walk 31
Wotton-under-Edge and the Tyndale Monument continued

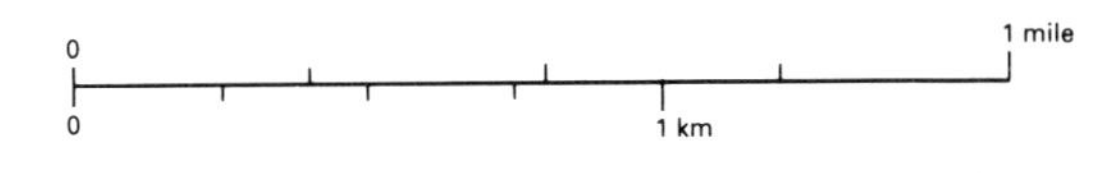

1 *Use the car park signposted near the monument. Walk back to the monument and continue west up the B4508 to Tabernacle Pitch on the right.*

2 *Turn right and then around to the left at the church. Continue ahead at the end up the path to the road. Turn right to a track on the left signposted to Tyndale Monument.*

3 *Turn left, then take the right fork, following the yellow arrows with a white dot, to the next junction.*

4 *Continue ahead. Take the right-hand path at the next two forks to a* T-*junction. Turn right to a complex of tracks.*

5 *Turn left through the gate and continue to the monument. With the door at your back, bear slightly left downhill to a stile.*

6 *Continue on the path to a sunken track, then turn right. Cross the stile to the left of the gate and continue across the field to a dirt track. Pass through the gate back to the complex junction of tracks.*

7 *Continue ahead to the left of the tree with the yellow arrow to a junction. Turn left, then shortly fork right up a minor path to a major track.*

8 *Go straight over to the next track. Continue ahead and, at the next track, turn left to the same junction as* **4**.

9 *Turn left and, after 100 yards (90 m), turn right down the track beside the field to the road.*

10 *Turn left, then shortly right along the path to Coombe Hill. Turn right at the track down to a stile. Continue to the corner of the fence.*

11 *Bear half-left downhill to the fence. Turn left and cross the stiles on the right. Continue down to the road and turn right back into the village.*

Walk 32

BATH AND THE KENNET AND AVON CANAL

7 miles ($11\frac{1}{4}$ km) Moderate; one climb

The walker is left to explore the centre of Bath for himself/herself as time and inclination permit. Instead, this route follows the Kennet and Avon Canal as it loops around Bathampton to the east of the city.

Canals are often associated with industrial grime and dirt, but here the waterway is flanked by most agreeable scenery, and the tow-path makes for very easy walking. The route then climbs Claverton and Bathampton Down, past the University to lead to a wonderful view of the honey-coloured stone buildings of the city.

A It is quite probable that early humans knew of the hot springs here, but the salt marsh that existed then prevented any permanent settlement.

The town was founded in the first century by the bath-loving Romans, attracted by the unfailing daily supply of 250 000 gallons (1 125 000 l) of water heated to 120 °F (49 °C).

The town of Aquae Sulis grew up around the baths. The buildings soon fell into disrepair after the Romans left, however, and, by the time the Saxons arrived after their victory at Dyrham in AD 577, the town was in an advanced state of decay. Nevertheless, it was obviously an important site, for Offa founded an abbey in AD 760, and King Edgar was crowned here in AD 973.

After almost destroying it, the Normans rebuilt the city, including a substantial cathedral – the present abbey only occupies the site of its nave. The city continued to profit from its renowned waters but it was not until after royal patronage in 1702 that Bath began its new era as a fashionable leisure and health resort. One man in particular, Richard (Beau) Nash, helped to mould the Georgian city. He it was who built the Assembly Rooms, the theatres, and controlled the gambling. It was during this period that many of the city's famous buildings were built, including the elegant Royal Crescent and the Circus.

By 1800, though, Bath had greatly declined as a fashionable centre, developing instead into a more industrial city.

B The canal was built to form a direct waterway between Bristol and London. It was designed to take 60-ton barges, and its 40-feet (12-m) width was unusually large for the time. Work was begun in 1794 to link the Kennet navigation at Newbury with the Avon at Bath, and it was completed in 1810, having cost around one million pounds.

East-bound cargo included coal and Bath stone, while timber, grain, and other agricultural produce made their way west. In 1848 360 000 tons of freight passed along the canal, but the waterway eventually became derelict after it was purchased by the Great Western Railway in 1852.

C Every time a boat passed through the seven (now six) locks to drop down into the River Avon, the canal lost thousands of gallons of water. To solve this problem, Rennie designed a pump capable of raising 100 000 gallons (450 000 l) an hour from the Avon into the canal 46 feet (14 m) above it. The pump was operated by a 16-foot (5-m) waterwheel driven by the river, and was in virtually continuous use for 140 years until it was damaged in 1952. It has since been fully restored.

D Forming something of a contrast with nearby Georgian England, the American Museum houses exhibits of American domestic life from the seventeenth to the nineteenth centuries. There are also Wild West and Indian collections.

Over

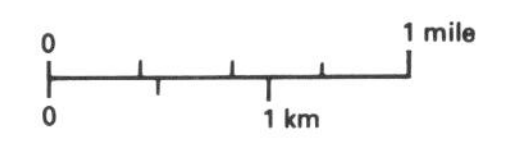

1 *Park in the city or in Sham Castle Lane (off Cleveland Walk, the connecting road between North Road and Bathwick Hill). Descend to the bottom of the lane and turn right to the main road.*

2 *Double back left along the path, turn right to cross the canal, then descend to the tow path and turn left. Follow the tow path for 3½ miles (5½ km).*

3 *Leave the canal by the pump information board and turn right on to the lane. Cross the canal and continue up to the A36. Turn left for 200 yards (180 m).*

4 *Turn right to Claverton Down and turn right into the private car park just past the American Museum. Go straight on to the gate and pass through the hedge on the left into the playing field.*

5 *Turn right and follow the hedge. Cross the stile into Bushey Norwood and walk to the left of the wire fence. Turn left just before the hedge and follow the path to a kissing gate in the corner of the field.*

6 *Go through the gate and turn left at the junction ahead. Follow the path along the edge of the golf course. Carry straight on over the bridleway to North Road as far as a gap in the wall.*

7 *Turn right across the golf course, and, after 200 yards (180 m), turn left and descend to Sham Castle.*

8 *Take the path in front of the castle down through the woods, across the drive, and through the gate opposite. Go straight down the field to the road.*

9 *Turn right, then left, after 200 yards (180 m), turn left through a gate. Go down the field, through the alleyway, and cross the road into Sham Castle lane opposite.*

Walk 33
DYRHAM AND HINTON HILL
2¼ miles (3½ km) Easy; some mud

This may be only a short walk but it is packed with history. Dyrham is a small village but the church contains the famous brass of Sir Maurice Russel and his wife.

The historical importance of Hinton Hill is much greater than the hillfort and lynchets suggest. As you walk past the hill or stand in the fort, you can almost visualize the British struggling uphill against the Saxons on the hilltop.

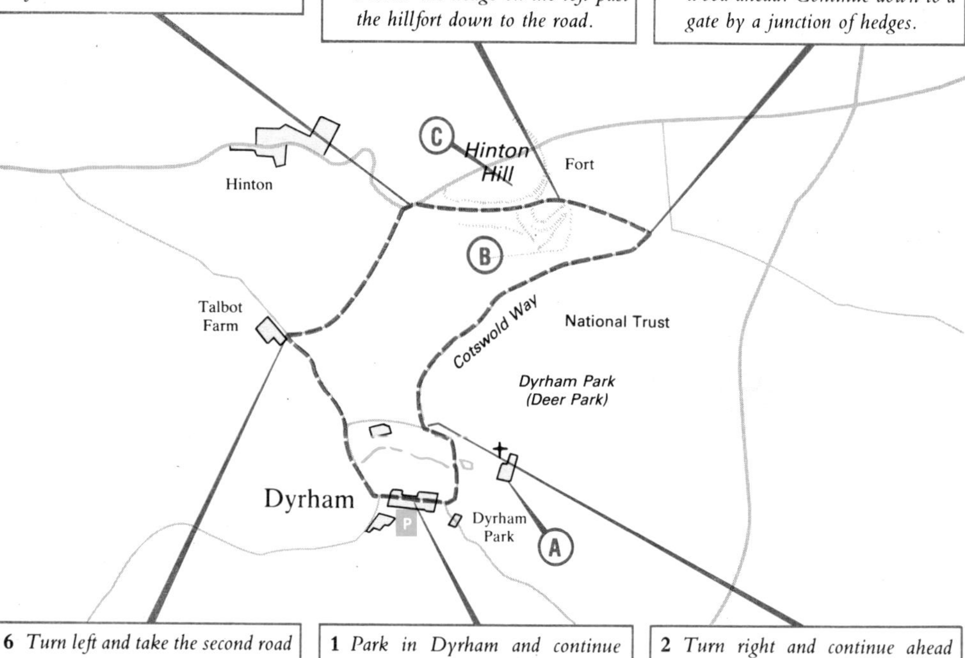

1 *Park in Dyrham and continue uphill past the old post office to the small green. Turn left, past Dyrham House, to a marked bridleway on the right.*

2 *Turn right and continue ahead through the gate. Follow the waymarked path to a gate at the road.*

3 *Turn back sharp left and head towards the left-hand edge of the wood ahead. Continue down to a gate by a junction of hedges.*

4 *Cross the stile beside the gate and continue to the right of the hedge. Follow the hedge on the left past the hillfort down to the road.*

5 *Turn left for 50 yards (45 m) then turn left again to the next junction.*

6 *Turn left and take the second road on the left back to the car.*

A Dyrham Park was rebuilt at the end of the seventeenth century by William Blathwayt, then Secretary of State. Repton's landscaping was replaced by a deer park in the nineteenth century. It is a National Trust property.

B These low banks are the remains of a system of strip lynchets, probably Medieval in age. The terraces eased cultivation by creating areas of flatter land in otherwise sloping ground.

C In AD 577 the Saxons occupied the old hillfort and defeated three British kings, thereby capturing Gloucester, Cirencester, and Bath, and effectively ousting the British into Wales and Cornwall.